CHEF JAY LITTMANN

HOW TO GET FROM THERE TO HERE

ONE MAN'S TRIUMPH OVER ADDICTIONS, OBESITY, AND BEING DOWN-AND-OUT

EMERALD
BOOK CO.

Published by Emerald Book Company
Austin, TX
www.emeraldbookcompany.com

Distributed by Emerald Book Company

For ordering information or special discounts for bulk purchases, please contact Emerald Book Company at PO Box 91869, Austin, TX 78709, 512.891.6100.

Design and composition by Greenleaf Book Group LLC
Cover design by Greenleaf Book Group LLC

Publisher's Cataloging-In-Publication Data
(Prepared by The Donohue Group, Inc.)

Littmann, Jay.
  How to get from there to here : one man's triumph over addictions, obesity, and being down and out / Jay Littmann.

  p. ; cm.

  ISBN: 978-1-934572-39-9

1. Littmann, Jay. 2. Cooks--Biography. 3. Addicts--Biography. 4. Overweight persons--Biography. 5. Poor--Biography. 6. Diabetics--Biography. I. Title.

TX649.L58 A3 2010
641.5092   2009944153

Part of the Tree Neutral™ program, which offsets the number of trees consumed in the production and printing of this book by taking proactive steps, such as planting trees in direct proportion to the number of trees used: www.treeneutral.com

TreeNeutral

Printed in the United States of America on acid-free paper.

10 11 12 13 14 10 9 8 7 6 5 4 3 2 1

First Edition

To Monica, Jacob, and Isaiah,
the most important people in my life.

Money is not an end all. Personal relationships—with your lover or your spouse, your children, your friends, and your family—are the most important things in life. It is a paradox, however, that you must almost always alienate the people in those relationships to achieve real success, yet you cannot be truly satisfied unless you are able to achieve—or at least to give it your best shot to achieve—whatever your personal goals may be, and in turn be able to share that satisfaction to achieve the best personal relationships with those you love.

—Chef Jay Littmann

PREFACE

WHY DID I WRITE this book?

For the money? No. Most writers probably have a better chance of getting rich by hitting the lottery than by writing. The main reason I wrote *How to Get from There to Here* is because I came out of the pits of hell to have an incredible life, and I did it without any particular talent or skills, with no money, and with average intelligence, and you can too.

It doesn't matter if you are a drug addict or an alcoholic, if you have no money or a lot of money. (Actually, it is an advantage if you don't have any money because, chances are, you're a lot more motivated to succeed.) You can achieve anything you want in life if you want it badly enough, are willing to do the legwork, and put your faith in God. You want to beat your addictions? You want that fancy sports car, the big house, wife, family, or a great body? You can have it all; because if I did it, so can you.

In the coming chapters I am going to tell you how I did it and share some tools to help you. This book is your first tool, and the second is confidence and the belief that you can have an incredible life too.

ACKNOWLEDGMENTS

FIRST OF ALL I would like to thank my wife, Monica, who loved me fat and in shape, poor and not so poor, and everything in between.

Next, I want to thank my sons, Isaiah and Jacob, who make me realize every time I see them what's important in life.

I want to thank my parents, Michael and Carol, who did the best that they could and always supported me and provided food and shelter when I needed it most. Thanks to my brothers and sister, who I put through hell as we were growing up. Thanks to my Aunt Linda, who always has an open ear when I need it.

Thanks to Karen Schroeder and Alfonso Ramirez, who treat my company as if it were their own, which has allowed me the time to write this book. I would also like to thank Kate Silver, who wrote an article for the *Las Vegas Weekly*, which motivated me to finally complete this book.

Finally, I'd also like to thank my customers and distributors of the Tri-O-Plex products who have stuck with me all these years.

NOTE FROM THE AUTHOR

SOME NAMES AND IDENTIFYING details in this book have been altered. I have done my best to accurately describe my life from my point of view. Conversations and quoted material that appear within the following pages are not a word-for-word representation of past exchanges; rather, they are meant to capture the spirit of what was said.

CHAPTER 1

IF YOU WERE TO ask me to pinpoint when I hit rock bottom, I'd tell you to pull up a chair. I hit enough rock bottoms to fill the Grand Canyon, and every time I'd creep toward the top, gravity just kept pulling me back.

My low points have run the gamut. You'd need to multiply them by about a dozen if you wanted to count all the things I've managed to black out. My criminal history, alone, is practically a laundry list. I've fled the police and had a cop hold a loaded gun to my head. I've tried breaking into a house in a desperate search for drugs. I've committed check fraud. I've committed regular fraud. I've stolen from my own parents. I've dealt drugs. I've gotten my kid brother to deal drugs. I've been in jail a handful of times—and should have been there more. The list goes on and on—all with the underlying theme of being drunk and/or high, or trying to get that way.

Oh, I'd thought about quitting—thought about it until the next beer was in front of my face, or the next line was in front of my nose. But there was always something better to do than getting sober.

One day, though, something changed. It was a Sunday, and I'd been up for days freebasing. That's when you take cocaine, mix it with baking soda, and melt it down and smoke it. It's extremely addictive and had been my drug of choice at the time. That is, until I was coming down from it. I was down so low that day that being dead actually sounded better than being alive.

I'm done, I said to myself. *Done.*

As the fog parted, I looked at my life for what it was, and I realized it wasn't much. I'd been living in Cape Cod, and believe me, my stay hadn't been all lighthouses and lobsters. When I first arrived there, I crashed on a cot at a friend's house until I found a job as a bouncer at a bar. Then I rented a place above the bar and was happy to be within stumbling distance of my job. Eventually, even that stumbling became too much of an inconvenience, and I stopped showing up for work.

I was floating by on unemployment and making a few extra bucks off hustling drugs, using the proceeds so I could get high on cocaine all night then wait for the closest liquor store to open at 8:00 in the morning to buy beer. I drank until I passed out. And then I'd wake up and do it all over again. Somehow, the uselessness of that managed to escape me at the time. A lot escaped me, actually.

But not the fact that I stank—literally. I couldn't even remember the last time I had showered. Between freebasing and drinking enough to take down an elephant, I'd lost the ability to care about things like cleanliness.

I didn't know much, but I knew this: I just couldn't go on like that. I wasn't sure where I was headed, but I knew that the state I was in scared me.

Saying to myself that I was done wasn't enough, though. I'd learned over the years that I was fickle. I'd always been my own best salesman and my own worst enemy. Which is why one moment, on that very same miserable Sunday, I could emphatically tell myself *I'm done*, and the next moment walk into the 19th Hole and belly up to the bar and order a beer. Usually, this was where things started to get better, or at least I would start to feel "normal." But something was wrong.

I took a pull off the cold, hard bottle, and for the first time in my life, I actually meant what I was saying: I was done.

I just can't do this anymore, I said to myself. *I can't.*

I turned and walked out.

I don't know what gave me the strength to quit on that day in May 1991, but I do know I'd gained some footing. It was the first step, the hardest step, admitting that my life was unmanageable and I was powerless over drugs and alcohol. It wouldn't be the last time that I would find opportunity in adversity. For decades to come, I would continue to struggle and find that the discomfort that comes with change and hard work is actually worth savoring. Without it, I wouldn't have my family or the successful business I built.

◆

We always seemed so normal from the outside. If you were to meet my family on the street in Everett, Massachusetts, during the years when I was growing up, you'd think we were a regular, middle-class Jewish family. My dad was a hospital administrator, and my mom stayed home raising my sister, my two brothers, and me—the oldest of their four children.

While our family portraits were all smiles, life within the walls of our home was less rosy. Look closer and you would see me, a rough-and-tumble kid with brown hair and bright blue eyes, overweight by age five, hiding behind the delicious home-cooked meals of my mother to avoid confrontation with my alcoholic father. All of us kids knew not to even try to get near Dad before he had had his first drink after work. That was when he was meanest. My mother would pretty much leave my father to himself while he drank his first few drinks and discuss any pressing subjects afterward. He'd become a little calmer as the night and the drinks wore on—and the drinks *always* wore on. He would drink whiskey and ginger ale until he went to bed, or passed out.

As bad as it sounds, the passing out was always a blessing for the whole family because that meant he'd leave us alone. As if it wasn't enough that the kids at school made fun of me for being fat, I'd have to come home and take it from my own father too.

As his oldest child, I always felt like I was his biggest disappointment. As far as he was concerned, I couldn't do anything—even dress myself—right.

"Where's your belt? You look like a slob," was his almost daily refrain. Dad seemed to despise everything about me, from the way I talked, to my weight, to the way I carried myself.

My mom was the opposite. A typical Jewish mother, she doted on her four children and gave us all that she could, wanting us to be the best we could be. She pretty much let my father keep to himself, although I do recall her intervening occasionally on behalf of her children. It's like she was trying to make up for everything old Dad was lacking.

Always the loving and nurturing one, Mom was the one who encouraged me to eat, eat, eat! I know her heart was in the right place. The problem was, while her homemade crown roast always seemed to make me feel better, it didn't exactly help my waistline or my reputation.

Not that it ever stopped me. I was a kid—a fat kid—and I acted like one. Food made me happy, so I ate it, whenever and wherever I could, even if I knew it was going to get me in trouble. I remember the time we were on a family vacation in Cape Cod. It still stings to think about it. It wasn't the beaches or the family fun that became the most memorable part of the trip. It was the humiliation.

My parents had invited some family and friends down to visit. One morning I poured myself a big bowl of cereal. I was about eight years old and still not skilled at getting the perfect cereal-to-milk ratio. So, when I had finished eating my breakfast, a pool of milk still sat in the bottom of my cereal bowl. For some reason, my father took it personally. It was more than he could handle, and he got mad—real mad. He scolded me for wasting food.

"Ya gonna just throw that away?" he snarled.

I was stunned into silence, as was everyone else. As friends and family looked on he ordered me to take a large glass from the cupboard, pour the leftover milk into it, and drink it. I did it. I drank that room-temperature milk, and as I swallowed it I also swallowed my anger and what was left of my pride. I felt like a dog that had just had an accident and his owner was rubbing his face in it while all the other adults looked on, squirming.

My dad also used to spank my brothers and me as part of his discipline. I don't recall him spanking my sister at all, maybe because she was female and a whole lot better behaved. I can't say I always blamed him, but that never took the sting away. The thing about physical abuse is that it's never just about the hitting. That part's not so bad. It's the psychological stuff that really burrows down into you. For me, the biggest thing was repression. My dad could beat the living hell out of me, and I never fought back. Ever. I'd sit there in silence, and I'd take it. I'd shake and I'd wince, but I'd take it. Then my anger would build and build for days and weeks, like a giant buildup of steam searching for an outlet.

Generally speaking, my outlet took the form of my little brothers and sister. Whenever my parents left the house, I'd find some way to pick a fight with them, or they'd start something with me. We were kids, and fighting was what we saw all the time with our dad. So given free rein, our house practically turned into a WWF ring—lamps would get tossed, vases smashed. Even the sturdier things like beds and doors were no match for the four of us. And the instant that something would break, we all knew we were done for. Dad would come home eventually. I think the wait for the inevitable beating was maybe as torturous as the beating itself. The memory of that kind of anxiety still brings a hollow, metallic taste of fear to my mouth.

When he finally got home, we'd all watch, wide-eyed, as he assessed the damage. The outcome was always totally unpredictable. Dad's reaction hardly had anything to do with the seriousness of what we'd done; it had more to do with how much he'd had to drink that night. We were really in for it when we could smell that sweet scent of whiskey before he'd barely made it through the door. That's when the belt would come off. As the oldest, I always seemed to get a few extra licks, just because. And as that belt *fwapped* down, and I fought off the hot, humiliated, angry tears, one thought would go through my mind: *I deserve it*. That's one thing my dad instilled in me, anyway. I deserved it.

When I was about ten years old, we moved from Everett to Newton. My father had come into some money and wanted to invest it in a bigger house and a new life in a better part of town. He figured it was time to upgrade our status.

The money had actually come from my paternal grandfather, who was one of perhaps four top heart specialists in the 1950s and 1960s. I never knew David Littmann, M.D., that well. He was pretty distant and cold as far as the family was concerned, not unlike my father. But when it came to medicine, he was a star. He improved the practice of medicine, especially the diagnosis of heart and lung problems, and served for years as an associate clinical professor of medicine at Harvard Medical School, which was where he invented the Littmann stethoscope. The 3M Company eventually bought that stethoscope from my grandfather and hired him as a consultant. Lucky for us, he wanted to share the wealth.

The big homes and Cadillacs of Newton were a change from our former blue-collar neighborhood for all of us. Unfortunately, despite the new setting, some things never changed.

I recall one particular night; dinner seemed to be off to a good start. We were all taking turns telling one another about what happened in our day, the way dinner should be. When it was my turn, I shared that my teacher had told the class that the average household produces four full bags of trash per week. I had found that interesting, so I reiterated the fact. I wasn't making a judgment call, or even comparing our trash-bag count to the average.

Well, it was too much for Dad. I could see the telltale signs of a meltdown right off: his face flushed, his eyebrows rose up like angry caterpillars, and his eyes almost popped out of his head.

Then came the screaming.

"No teacher is going to tell ME how many bags of trash I should have!" he belted out.

The screaming always made me flinch, no matter the warning signs. I remember just sitting there—cowering—wishing, praying for him to calm down. The wrath behind his words was so strong it was like a punch to my gut.

Then, horror of horrors, he threatened to march into that school and tell that teacher exactly how he felt. My face reddened at the thought of it, my fists clenched under the table.

I tried not to act upset—that would only egg him on. So I stared at my plate and quietly continued eating, hoping that somehow my mother's sweet-and-sour meatballs would deliver me from the pain and self-loathing, would squelch the anger I was feeling toward old Dad. I hated myself for making him that angry, and I hated him for making me feel that way. Now, on top of everything else, I had to worry about him making a scene at a school where the kids already taunted me. I worried about it all night, and for the days that followed.

Maybe it was just the whiskey and ginger ale talking, because he never did show up at school.

♦

By the time I was twelve, the ingredients of my life were coming together to make a toxic combination. I didn't fit in at school, I didn't fit in at home, and the less I fit in, the more I hated myself. For pretty much all of those twelve years, food had been my No. 1 escape. But now that I was getting older, other temptations started making themselves available. Turns out there are far more effective ways to indulge yourself than eating a sweet-and-sour meatball.

I ran with a core group of friends: Johnny, Mitch, Buff, and Franx. We were constantly restless, the five of us, and constantly bored. And what do a bunch of kids do when they've got a lot of time on their hands and they're not real happy? Anything they could find that would make them feel different from who they really were. For us, that meant drinking.

It began with weekends. Our parents' supply became our supply. We'd find out whose folks were out for the night and then steal their liquor and get drunk. From the very first time I tried it—beer, whiskey, all of it, it didn't matter—I loved the way it made me feel. As a kid who was nearly 75 pounds overweight, I discovered that alcohol was the first thing I'd tasted or experienced that made me forget I was fat. Instead, I felt like a normal goofy kid, a kid who was a part of something. I mean, with this at my lips, I didn't have to think about the kids at school making fun of me or my father berating me. Drinking made me happy, it made me not think. The only downside was the hangover. But I figured every up had its down, and this up was well worth it.

Drinking soon became our favorite activity. Before long, our parents' liquor cabinets were depleted and it was clear that we were going to have to find some kind of supply outside of our families. We didn't have a lot of options. Our one hope was Franx. He was a heavy kid too, but whereas my heaviness translated into chubby cheeks on a husky boy, his weight made him look much older. So we sent him into the liquor store and kept our fingers crossed. Believe it or not, it worked. He wasn't even a teenager, and he was able to buy beer. And man, were we grateful.

Our main hangout was at the Charles River skating rink, where we'd meet up with other kids from the area. I had never been much of a skater when I was sober, so I didn't even bother trying while I was drinking. I'd just sit around, drink, shoot the shit, look at the girls. The girls never seemed to look back at me, but I guess I couldn't blame them.

It was here that I smoked my first joint. From that first puff it was like I'd found my calling. This—*this*—was what I was meant to do. I loved marijuana. Loved it so much I practically convinced myself that I'd discovered a wonder drug. I loved being high even more than I loved drinking, and that was saying a lot. Pot calmed me down, made me feel better about myself. There was this whole communal aspect to smoking a joint. I'd sit with a group of people and pass it around, sharing the same experience. Sometimes we'd talk, other times we'd just inhale, hold the smoke in until we just had to take a breath, and then exhale, coughing as the gray haze left our mouths. It was a bonding experience like I'd never had.

Plus, I didn't have to worry about smoking too much and being hung over. As far as I was concerned, the only sort of negative side to pot was that it gave me the munchies, which, to me, wasn't such a bad thing. Like I said, I was a big fan of eating.

Between the drinking and the pot I actually started making more friends and feeling like I fit in with my seventh-grade class. All my life I'd felt awkward around my classmates. I didn't know what to say to them or how to act. Now I finally felt like I had something in common with the other kids. It was like we were some kind of secret club that was daring enough to do something our parents may well have killed us for.

It wasn't long before pot became my favorite pastime. I smoked morning, noon, and night. Sometimes the guys would join me, other times I'd hang out with the school potheads. After a while I didn't even care if there were friends to smoke with or not. I loved getting high by myself. I'd just lie there and light up and wait to feel like I was walking on clouds, not giving a damn about anything but feeling good.

In hindsight, it was probably about the worst thing in the world for an already fat kid to do because it just made me lazy. I'd lie around like a baked potato, staring at the television. I loved the uselessness of it all. It took me out of my own head to places that were far more enjoyable. I'd sit and stare for hours at a time. It was actually kind of funny: my dad had accused me of being lazy my whole life, and now it was like a self-fulfilling prophecy—I really was lazy, and I didn't want it any other way.

It was always easy to find more pot. There were kids all over school who sold it; you just had to know who to talk to, and you had to have the money for it. That was the only hard part. I wasn't even old enough to have a job. How was I supposed to make enough money to support a growing drug habit?

The answer was usually Mom and Dad. I would sneak bills of all sizes out of my mom's wallet. Occasionally, she would notice that something was missing. I'd watch her pick up her purse and a mystified look would come over her face. One day I even saw her counting her money. But she never did say anything. Not even when one of her gold bracelets went missing. I'd taken it to a jeweler and used the cash to get more pot.

I don't know how I got it past them. I liked to think I was subtle, but when you're that high you can only be so subtle. I had a constant supply of Visine to try and keep the red out of my eyes, and I did my best to act normal around them. But the truth is, they were pretty naïve. My mom kept busy in the kitchen, and my dad was detached and unconcerned. So it wasn't hard to go unnoticed in the Littmann household.

Their ignorance didn't last as long as I'd hoped it would, however. I'm still not sure what it was, exactly, that tipped them off. I think it had something to do with a movie they had watched called *The Death of Richie*. It was one of those public-service-announcement style made-for-TV movies about a teenager's spiral into drug addiction. After watching that, their antennas went straight up. They started looking at me differently, watching me when they didn't think I was looking. Then came the uncharacteristic questions and curiosity. It was completely out of character, and it totally weirded me out.

But it didn't prepare me for the day I came home from school and found my stash was gone. I looked behind my dresser drawers (my hiding place), and it was empty. I felt all around my dresser, looked under it, looked behind other drawers, and it was nowhere to be found. Gone.

They found me out, I thought to myself. *Damn.*

I started pacing, breathing heavily, doing all those normal things you do when you're panicking. I circled the house, and that's when I saw it on the kitchen table: two bags of pot, my metal pipe, and my glass pipe. It was all there, right in front of me. There might as well have been a neon sign above it flashing the word "CAUGHT."

I stiffened, waiting for my parents' screams. But they never came. I almost wish they had, because what followed was worse. I watched as the tears ran down my mother's face. Then she just started bawling; bawling because of me, what I had done, who I had become. It made me feel terrible. My dad wasn't much better. He just sat there in stony silence. I could actually feel the weight of their disappointment crushing me.

Even so, I wasn't sorry for using drugs. I was sorry that I'd been caught. At least they hadn't yet noticed that I'd been stealing from them.

CHAPTER 2

WHEN I TURNED THIRTEEN I became a man. That's what they told me, anyway. That's the age, according to Jewish tradition, that signifies the transition from childhood to adulthood and is celebrated with a bar mitzvah (for boys) or a bat mitzvah (for girls). If you were to judge my maturity level by the way I handled the ceremony and the party afterward, you'd be right to question just how manly I was.

I hadn't attended too many other bar and bat mitzvahs prior to my own. Being overweight and unpopular tends to keep a guy off the invite list. Plus, I just wasn't that into religion. I'd been forced to attend Hebrew school four days a week for two hours a day (plus Sunday school) since fourth grade, and frankly, with the discovery of my new extracurricular activities, I had things I would rather be doing.

Which is probably why my bar mitzvah performance was less than stellar. Nearly two hundred people attended, and as is the tradition, I stood at the altar and began reciting a section from the Torah. It was something I'd been practicing for months, but somehow, right in the middle of it, I forgot my lines. I stumbled, searching my brain for what I was supposed to be saying, and came up with nothing. Seconds seemed like hours, and after an uncomfortable silence, the rabbi skipped ahead to the next part of the ceremony. I felt like a failure for about the millionth time in my life.

But I didn't let it get me down for long. To my friends and me, the real meaning of the bar mitzvah was located at the open bar during the party that followed. While a band that sounded kind of like Captain and Tennille livened up the night and distracted our parents, my friends and I snuck away so we could get drunk and high. By that time, my flubbed lines felt like they were a million miles away.

◆

Soon after my bar mitzvah, Buff and his parents invited Johnny, Franx, and me to go with them on a trip to Peru. I had a bunch of money I'd gotten as gifts for my bar mitzvah, so my parents allowed me to go and pay for it on my own. It was my first trip away from my family, and my first time ever to leave the country. If this was what manhood meant, I was already a fan.

The plane trip to Lima took fifteen hours. I don't remember too much about the flight, or even the hotel. What I do remember is discovering that Peru had no minimum drinking age. We were thirteen years old and we could drink, legally! The guys and I whooped it up, imagining all the drinks we'd order over the next few days. Then we discovered it was as easy as calling up room service. So we ordered a bunch of beer, downed about seven each, and passed out. This was gonna be the best vacation ever.

The next night we decided to check out a club. The three guys and I wandered the streets of Lima looking for a place that wasn't too far from our hotel. We settled on a dark, seedy place downtown. It smelled like old smoke and stale beer, and I didn't know it at the time, but that smell would later become an important backdrop to my life.

Walking in, I half expected that the heads would all turn toward us, like you'd see when the villain walks into a saloon in an old Western. But that didn't happen. The four of us were just about the only ones there.

We grabbed a table and started drinking shots of some kind of Inca liquor that was stronger than anything I had ever tried—before or since. (The closest thing to it is Bacardi 151, at 151 proof.) At first, it tasted like poison, but once I got past the first shot or two, it wasn't so bad. The guys seemed to like it too, and the more we drank, the rowdier we got. We were being pretty loud when a few ladies decided to join us. New as we were to being teenagers, with raging hormones and very little experience, this about made our night.

The women were older, and not exactly the kind of girls you'd take home to meet Mom. Their clothes didn't cover too much, and we were getting all kinds of views of all kinds of body parts as the night went on. They didn't speak English, and we didn't speak any Spanish, but none of us seemed bothered by the language barrier. I imagine that because we were young Americans they assumed we had unlimited funds from our parents, and were looking to party.

They got their wish. The ladies kept ordering drinks and putting them on our tab. And the more they kissed, touched, and flirted with us, the less we cared about our growing bill. Our minds were elsewhere.

After a few hours of this, I think the owner of the bar started to get skeptical about how we were going to pay for it all. We'd been drinking pretty heavily, and we were kids, after all. So he came over and demanded money. By that time, the evening's events were pretty fuzzy. But I clearly remember our tab came to the equivalent of nearly $600. Six. Hundred. American. Dollars. No wonder the guy was skeptical. What thirteen-year-old brings that kind of money to a Peruvian club? None in our group had. And the women? Well, they'd chosen that opportune moment to disappear.

What could we do? Calling our parents was not an option. But . . . That's when Franx, who'd always been the fast talker and problem solver in the group, piped up. He explained to the club owner that we had the money, but it was back in our hotel room. He offered to go back and get it. The owner agreed, under the condition that we all stayed put until Franx returned with the cash.

Franx darted out of the bar, leaving us sitting there, helpless and drunk. The reality of the situation killed our buzzes, and we were all starting to feel the signs of an early hangover as we waited and waited for him to come back. It felt like forever, but it was actually just an hour until Franx returned, victorious. He'd had enough stashed away for the trip that he was able to cover the bar tab, and he became, once again, our hero. We all stumbled back to the hotel to sleep off the rough night.

If you'd told me that that was just a glimpse of the danger to come, I probably would have stayed in bed the next day. Instead, I joined the group on a trip to Cuzco to visit Machu Picchu, located high in the Andes Mountains.

A few of us—Buff and his brother Daniel and his friend Greg—decided to climb the mountain to the top. We expected it to be a fairly easy climb because there were these rock formations that wound to the top like a giant stairway. Even so, I think I surprised the gang when I said I was going to go along. To look at me then, you wouldn't have thought I had any interest in any sort of exertion. But when I put my mind to something, my will alone is enough to propel me along.

Out of shape, overweight, and hung over, I soon realized the climb was tougher than it looked. Once I got to the top of the eight-thousand-foot peak, I was out of breath and a little bit dizzy, but nonetheless exhilarated and relieved to have made it to the top. The view across Peru was stunning—so stunning that I somehow managed to stop paying attention to where I was walking and I slipped on one of the stones. The effect was like a landslide—one stone became many, and suddenly I was about to tumble off the mountain. My hands caught hold of something solid on my way down, and thankfully, Daniel heard the commotion.

"Hey, guys, Jay's falling!" he cried out.

They rushed over, and Buff, who was the closest to me, grabbed my arm and dragged me back on to solid ground. I was stunned, silent, gasping for breath. It wasn't until Daniel proclaimed, "*Geez*, that was a close one," that I realized just how serious the situation could have been. If Buff hadn't been right there, I could have easily fallen to my death.

The rest of the visit was a blur. We'd all been humbled—for the moment, at least—by the first two days and avoided any real risky behavior for the rest of the trip. Before I knew it, we were on our flight back to Boston. I didn't realize it then, but my first near-death experience wouldn't be my last. Not by any stretch.

♦

When I got back home I'd spent nearly all of my bar mitzvah money. I wasn't looking forward to returning to the same routine, where I stole from my parents to fuel my habit. Not that I'd had some sudden development of conscience or anything. It was more like my cravings were exceeding my supply, and the petty larceny just wasn't cutting it. I wanted more, and I knew if I was going to actually get more I'd have to start thinking like an entrepreneur. I would have to make money, somehow. I just wasn't sure how.

The answers all became clear when a friend introduced me to Robert the drug dealer. Robert was older than us, somewhere in his twenties. The guy looked pretty normal, and he seemed nice enough. He had long black hair and was a little rough around the edges; he always looked like he needed to shave. But what I really noticed was the yellow Corvette he drove. I'd always loved cars—the faster the better—and this one was pretty hot. I wanted what he had.

If I were to deal and make the kind of money Robert told me I could, I knew that someday I could afford a car like his too. I would also have all the drugs I ever wanted, right at my fingertips. Plus, it would make me important. It was mind-blowing to think about. I was so blinded by the green that I didn't even consider the fact that this guy still lived with his mom and that most of his life was spent smoking pot in his bedroom.

I left the meeting excited by the possibilities. I wanted this life, this freedom, this cash, and this continual drug access. I knew that most people, or at least people like my parents, considered selling drugs a highly risky business. To that, I said *pshaw*. I had no worries about getting caught or getting hurt or anything like that. I was a big kid. I'd be fine. I just knew it. As far as I was concerned there was no downside. Except, of course, that I didn't have enough money to buy a quarter-pound right then and open up my doors for business.

I told Johnny all about it, and he wanted in too. He was just as broke as I was, though, so we fell back on our most tried-and-true ways of scoring quick cash: we stole $120 from our parents. It was our "seed" money, enough to buy four ounces of pot, which we then divided into smaller portions. Only problem was we didn't have a scale. So we waited until it was dark and we broke into our high school and stole scales from the science department. We took them home and measured the pot into quarter-ounce and half-ounce bags, which we sold for $10 per quarter ounce.

It was an easier business than you might think. Everyone wanted to buy a bag. We sold it at school and at parties; anywhere we went our doors were open for business, and we were never wanting for clients. In the end, we could make a profit of about $40 if we sold all the stash. If you factored in my smoking about a half-ounce a week, the profits were even less impressive. But I liked the excitement, and for the first time in my life, I felt needed.

Somehow, through it all, I managed to keep my grades up. I knew I wanted to go to college to study business (I guess you could say my childhood sales experience was like getting a crash course in that), and I knew that I had to work hard to make that happen. I was a responsible addict is one way of putting it. I limited my drinking and drugging to the weekends. I still smoked pot every day, but I held off on lighting up until after my homework was completed. As bad kids go, I was still a pretty good kid.

I was also a pretty experimental kid. Now that I was selling pot I had a constant supply. To someone with an addict's mentality, however, that still wasn't enough. I wanted more, always more. I'd heard some friends talking about Quaaludes. They're pills that act like a sedative and mus-cle relaxant, and they were becoming pretty popular in the 1970s. The way I understood it, I could basically feel drunk without the hangover, or the calories. What more could you ask for?

I bought some from my pot dealer and loved the sensation immediately. The "lude" was much stronger than pot and alcohol; I felt euphoric. I forgot about my weight problems, my family issues, and my awkwardness with girls. That was saying something.

By the time another year had rolled around, I'd had no luck with the opposite sex. Why would they want to be seen with a fat guy? What could I do for them? Try as I might to lose weight, it always came back. I'd managed to diet successfully a few times, shed a few pounds here, a couple sizes there, but I could never keep it off. The more weight I gained, the more I hated myself. Whether I was eating for emotional reasons or binging after getting high, overindulging was the real constant in my life.

♦

My sophomore year in high school my father quit drinking. He never gave us a concrete reason. We all just figured that he got sick of relying on something that was ruining his health. He said he was ready to become an active part of his life and family again. It was pretty insightful for him, considering. I hoped for some kind of miraculous turnaround and a newfound family closeness, but that didn't happen. He didn't become Ward Cleaver overnight.

At first, his sobriety was actually harder on my mother and us kids. He'd been a drunk for so long that he didn't know how to be sober, and we all seemed to get the brunt of it. He'd holler at the littlest thing, go off on us kids for God knows what. Everyone picked up on whatever warning signs we could and began treading more lightly than ever. Personally, I would tread lightly straight to the refrigerator.

Between my father and my weight, all of the problems of my youth were escalating the older I got. And the only thing that would make them go away was chemical in nature. Once I'd started downing Quaaludes it was like I'd opened a new door, and by the end of the school year, I was open to trying pretty much anything.

Hallucinogens came first. Something called purple microdot had been circulating in Newton. I wasn't sure if it was LSD, PCP, or a combination of both, and I didn't really care. If it was available, I was trying it.

To my surprise, I didn't like it that much. It made me see things that weren't there. I saw traces of the outlines of objects, and blurry images on the wallpaper seemed to move. It also made me feel paranoid. I could hear voices inside my head, and they freaked me out. I wanted to jump out of my own skin. Plus, every time I took it I felt stuck: the effects lasted for up to twenty-four hours, and I couldn't come down no matter how badly I wanted to. I would drink and drink and drink to try and make myself feel better, but the alcohol just didn't work when I was on that drug.

I also discovered something called blotter, which looked like a water spot on a piece of paper. Its effects were similar to the purple microdot, but a little less intense. Even if I didn't enjoy being on either drug, it was better than being straight. Like a true addict, I just kept taking them. I took them more than a dozen times, and the more I did it the worse the trip. I could feel the residual effects, and even when I wasn't tripping, my mind just felt . . . different. I don't know how else to describe it. I knew I was screwing myself up, but I didn't let that stop me. Like I said, my motto was "Even a bad drug is better than no drug." It was, at least, until the next one came along.

The next one was cocaine. As the hippies of the 1970s gave way to the glam rockers of the 1980s, the drug of choice also changed, and coke was everywhere—including up my own nose. Back then, we were told it wasn't addictive. Zoom ahead a few decades and we now know that's simply not the case. Not that any kind of scientific research would have stopped me when I was a teenager.

I didn't fall in love with coke immediately like I had with alcohol, pot, and Quaaludes; I developed more of a gradual appreciation for it. The first two times I snorted it I barely felt anything. But the third time I tried it, I felt as though I'd consumed about five hundred cups of coffee.

Really, really *good* coffee. After years of relying on depressants, I found this stimulant literally eye-opening. When I snorted coke, it gave me an edge and an alertness. Added to that, I could drink even more than usual without getting sick.

Cocaine was an expensive habit to develop, though; it sold for about $100 a gram back then. I actually think that's one of the things I liked most about it: the fact that I was willing to shell out so much cash for it gave me status. I also enjoyed the whole ritual surrounding it. Coke was an involved process that had to be learned. I would pour the chunky white powder out on a mirror and cut it with a razor blade to form a series of sleek, white lines. My preferred snorting tool was a rolled-up hundred-dollar bill. From there, the soft powder gave way to a slightly medicinal flavor that traveled up my nose and down my throat, numbing its path, and beyond.

As my drug habits grew more extravagant, I had to steer my career to be able to afford them. At fifteen years of age, I started dealing cocaine. You might think my job became more complicated, more dangerous at this point, but expanding my sales to include the harder stuff was seamless. I continued selling at parties and to students and still never had to do much marketing.

I myself was binging pretty regularly and often stayed up all night, even past sunrise. Because of the drugs, I was in a constant state of paranoia and financial strain. The more I used, the more I needed to use to achieve the same high. To battle the dehydrating effects of the cocaine I drank more beer than ever, and I started using downers, like barbiturates, to counterbalance the intensity of the high. It was like I was on a teeter-totter: I kept piling things on one side to bring me up and then on the other to take me back down, always in search of the proper balance, but never quite satisfied once I got there.

♦

It was during one of my binges that I got the idea of running away. I'm not sure what started the impulse. I think it was a combination of things:

my relationship with my parents, the desire to see my father actually worry, and the need to test whether, by leaving home, I also could find a way to leave myself behind. I was a big shot now, bringing in cash hand over fist. Usually the proceeds went right back into buying more drugs, but not this time. I wanted to do something drastic and spontaneous; heading to Miami just felt like the right move. Because that's the kind of things drug dealers do, right?

At the heart of it, really, I was seeking more of an escape than the drugs were allowing me. I was so emotionally and mentally gone at that point, leaving, physically, seemed like the only answer. I just wanted to stop being me. I thought that maybe if I were someplace else, I would feel better.

I got all dressed up in my suit and took a cab to the airport. I bought a one-way ticket to Miami. Once I got there, I ignored the pristine beaches, the glamorous clubs and restaurants, and the beautiful women. I was after the same thing I was always after.

I looked up someone I knew at the University of Florida. He was a friend of a friend, and I knew he could hook me up with drugs. I was right. I bought a half-ounce of cocaine and about fifty ludes, and after indulging in both, I spent some time wandering around campus. I decided I wanted a drink, but that was easier said than done for a fifteen-year-old.

Suddenly feeling out of my comfort zone—and blitzed out of my gourd—I wasn't sure what to do with myself. So I turned around and got a cab back to the airport. I wanted to go home. I still wasn't entirely sure what had drawn me here in the first place, but I knew it hadn't brought me the deliverance I'd hoped for.

I was so blasted on Quaaludes I almost missed my flight. But I managed to pull myself together and make it back to Boston. I hopped in a cab and convinced the driver to buy me a bottle of Jack Daniel's and a six-pack of Molson beer. By the time I got home, my parents hadn't even noticed I was gone. So much for causing them to worry!

I headed directly to my room, where I proceeded to drink the entire bottle of Jack, snort cocaine, and swallow a handful of Quaaludes. It was a combination my body was familiar with, but after my having gone at it all day, the volume must have been more than even I could handle. The room started spinning. I doubled over feeling sick, so sick.

I stumbled out of my room and told my father I'd taken too many pills. He gave me this look that was more disgust than concern. Without a word, he called the hospital where he worked and asked what he should do. They told him to bring me in. I think that in his mind that was about the worst thing they could have said. I could hear it in his curt response and the silence that followed.

He didn't say a word the whole drive there. I was still out of it, but I could sense my father's disgust. When we arrived at Beth Israel Hospital in Brookline, they put me on a stretcher. From there, I'm not sure what happened. I can't remember whether they pumped my stomach or if I threw up. They could have done just about anything at that point and I wouldn't have known.

They kept me overnight, and that was fine with me. Though I hadn't planned it out or anything, I think this episode was a subconscious cry for help, and everybody knew it. I figured once I got home, my life was going to change. And probably not for the better.

CHAPTER 3

WHEN THEY RELEASED ME from Beth Israel the next day, I was still out of it and in no shape to deal with the sea of emotions that hit when I got home. My mom was hunched over, tears streaming down her face, and it looked like she'd been like that for a while. I couldn't stand to see her cry, and now it seemed like it was becoming a regular thing. I wasn't sure what to do, though. I've never been good at dealing with emotions or handling emotional outbursts, so I just stood there awkwardly.

Very sadly she told me that she was afraid for my life. She brought up that movie again, *The Death of Richie*, and explained that she was terrified about what would happen to me, because at the end of the film the father shot the son. I think that movie had really been her only exposure to drugs, and she had no way to process what was happening to me. No wonder she was freaked out. Considering her son had just come home from a drug-fueled Miami trip and ended up in the emergency room, I guess her feelings were justified.

My dad was less emotional but more direct in his approach. He sat me down and demanded to know what was going on. I fessed up, told him about the drugs I'd been using, and then waited for the blows. Only the blows didn't come. He was more rational that day than he had been the day before. My unapproachable dad, of all people, understood all too well what I was going through. He'd recently begun attending recovery meetings, and I could see that they were actually helping him deal with his anger. I say that because I didn't flinch once during my confessional.

I think he was finally starting to see just how out of control I was—much like he had been for all those years. I was a little surprised when he asked a friend whom he'd met at one of his meetings to come over and stage an intervention. The idea was that they'd take me to a recovery meeting, I'd listen to all the horror stories of addiction, and they would make me realize that I wasn't alone and that this was where I needed to be. I gave them credit for trying. But they may as well have taken me to another planet. The thing Dad was forgetting was that until it was my choice, my decision, no intervention was going to stick. I just wasn't ready to quit. That was the bottom line.

In fact, the more my father did under the guise of helping me, the worse off I felt. It was like he was trying to make up for years of distance, but the closer he tried to get, the angrier I became. Years of unresolved issues felt like they were boiling under my skin, creating welts full of pain and anger, and every time he tried to get closer, those welts would flare up. I guess he thought he was trying the best he could, but for me it was already too little too late.

You would think that it would be easy for one addict to help another, but when it comes to being in the same family, it just doesn't work that way. What my dad needed to do was let me follow my own path, no matter how difficult that was. But that was something that would take him—and me—years to understand. So when he told me he thought we could benefit from therapy, I agreed to give it a try. By the end of the first session, we were practically at each other's throat. All the therapist did was inflame those giant welts even more.

See, as much as Dad was trying to help me, I'd recently learned of a family secret that hurt me even more than all those times he had called me "fat." A cousin told me about a stash of family money Dad had access to. The money came from my grandfather. I'd come to find out that when we moved from Everett to Newton, there had actually been a lot more money in play than the cash that financed our new home. When my grandfather sold the patent and business for his stethoscope to the 3M Company, he took the proceeds and, for tax purposes, divided them among himself, my father, my two cousins, and me (or so I was told). According to the bank documents, my cousins and I were supposed to be given access to the money when we turned eighteen. Except no one ever bothered telling me that.

Whatever my grandfather's reasoning, my share—which was substantial—had been put into a trust under my father's control. So the same day I learned that I had all of this money, I also learned that my father had already spent most of it. To add to that insult, I also found out that at one point Dad convinced my younger brother to pretend he was me. He forged my signature on one of the remaining stock certificates and then gave the cash to my father.

I felt ripped off, betrayed, and hurt. All my life I'd suspected my father's resentment of me, and now this proved it. I was like a second-class citizen in my own family, and now I knew that I wasn't paranoid to feel that way, I was being realistic. The therapist suggested that my destructive behavior had been exacerbated by this new discovery. He didn't try to justify my actions, just to analyze them. Me, I don't know. Maybe that betrayal had something to do with my worsening dependence on drugs and alcohol. But I didn't really care about *why* I had these tendencies. It was never about that. I just wanted to satisfy them. For years, my primary focus had been avoiding any kind of self-analysis and self-discovery and just trudging along. Getting drunk and high was just so much easier than any of that stuff. It was easier than therapy, that's for sure. Our first session also turned out to be our last.

My stubbornness only added to my parents' frustration. Nothing they did seemed to be making a difference, so they had me committed to the chemical dependency unit of Bournewood, a psychiatric hospital in Brookline. Soon after I got there I learned that I wasn't the first family member who had checked in to the facility. Years and years ago my maternal grandmother had been hospitalized there, more than once, for mental illness. She actually received electroshock therapy in an attempt to battle her depression.

Fortunately, I didn't receive such extreme treatment. Detox and counseling were my primary focus—or, at least, the primary focus for my counselors and doctor. That, and scare tactics.

They put me in a locked ward, surrounded by men who had a condition known as Wernicke-Korsakoff syndrome, or "wet brain." It's something caused by long-term alcoholism and affects people kind of like Alzheimer's does. To a seventeen-year-old kid who had never even spent real time away from home, it was terrifying. Glancing around, all I could see were shells of people, zombies incapable of conversation and totally unable to care for themselves.

I guess this was the hospital staff's way of showing me that if I kept up my damaging behavior this was where I was headed. It was heavy stuff, a little too much for me to handle. Rather than embrace their message, I went into self-preservation mode. All I wanted was to keep to myself and make it through the day without being noticed. I avoided eye contact as much as I could, but when the other patients weren't looking, I would take it all in.

One of the guys in the ward was like a robot. He couldn't think for himself or carry on a conversation, but he could carry out certain physical functions, like feeding himself and even playing pool. His brain seemed hardwired to remember particular things, but it was hit or miss as to which ones. The diaper he wore was a reminder of some of the lost functions.

The ward was pretty much a ballet of dysfunction. There was the guy who flat-out refused to eat, and the overweight, scary guy who silently stared out the window all day. Then there was the other fat guy in the ward who would get regular visits from some woman, and I accidentally caught a glimpse of them having sex in his room one day. That image took awhile to shake.

They all freaked me out for one reason or another. But the guy I would go out of my way to avoid was a black-haired, lanky man in his late fifties who was there for alcohol abuse. His treatment was pretty extreme—electroshock therapy. Rumor had it that it was because he was a pedophile with a taste for young boys.

During my first five days there I was exhausted. I had never realized the toll the drugs and drinking were taking on my body until I was forced to stop taking them. I couldn't seem to get enough sleep. After I checked in I basically slept three days straight. I'd wake up, still tired, night after night, day after day. My stomach was like a turbine it was so upset. Even though I knew that the chemicals were to blame for my feeling so low, I would have done anything for a beer or a line of coke.

To make things worse, there was hardly anything to do there. Whoever thought of putting a detoxing addict into a stiflingly boring environment surrounded by crazies was clearly off his meds. When I wasn't sleeping I tried to read, but I could barely concentrate on anything. I couldn't shake feeling betrayed by my parents, bored, and depressed. I was hit by a whole host of emotions, and I had nothing but time to really focus on them. Great.

I think five days went by before they moved me out of the locked ward and into another part of the hospital. This time they put me in a dormlike atmosphere and told me I could come and go as I pleased. It was comfortable, less sterile there. I didn't feel like I was in the nuthouse anymore. I was relieved to be away from the wet brains and in with people who were like me. That's where I met Chris and Darla, a couple of kids my age I could really relate to.

Chris was seventeen and had spent the past few months in jail for stealing cars and dealing drugs. A judge ordered the prison to release him so that he could get treatment in this facility. He wasn't exactly thrilled about his newfound sobriety, but he was relieved to be in a less restrictive environment. Darla was a thin and pretty blond girl, about sixteen years old, and like me, her parents had put her in here against her will.

We all went through the motions that the hospital required. We'd go see a doctor occasionally, for about ten minutes at a time, and we attended recovery meetings when they were available to us. But that was the only structure we were given.

That meant that Chris, Darla, and I had all sorts of free time to talk about the stuff we had in common: drug dealing, stealing, drugs, alcohol, and sex. Talking about it made us want it all the more. I mean it was bad. So one night, we decided to go for it.

We hatched a plan that, even in hindsight, was pretty brilliant. One of the other guys living there with us went around and collected whatever money anyone had. Then, while we were all playing basketball, he slipped off to a different part of the grounds. He hid until evening, knowing that the reduced number of counselors after dark would diminish the possibility of him being caught. When the sun went down, he ran.

He found a liquor store and bought a few bottles to bring back. We hid them under our beds and in drawers and discreetly took pulls off them when no one was looking. That bottle sure tasted sweet.

After a couple of days, though, the liquor had lost its charm and became nothing more than a tease. I would still sneak swigs off it, but they'd lost their zip. For years drinking just made me crave other things. It was no different now that I was in rehab. I wanted the hard stuff. I wanted some coke.

I arranged a drug deal. I knew a girl on the outside who needed a half-ounce of coke, so I told her to pick me up from the hospital. She followed my directions and drove us to pick up the coke. I cut it, meaning I took some out for myself to get high, and put some additives into it so it wouldn't look like any was missing. After one taste, I knew my entire night was spoken for. It was me and the white powder, together at last.

The only place I could think to go was my parents' house. It was late enough that they should be asleep, leaving me all the privacy I needed. So the girl dropped me off and I went directly to my room and made up for lost time. What followed was an all-out binge until the sun rose and I heard my parents getting up. Reality set in, and my father found me. At a loss for what to do, he took me back to the hospital.

I figured I'd get a lecture when I got back there, but what was waiting to greet me was worse than any words. They put me right back into the locked ward and told me to take off my clothes. One of the staff pulled on a pair of disposable gloves and performed my first cavity search. There are no words to describe the humiliation of that experience. When they put me back into the locked ward with the wet brains, all I could do was curl up in the fetal position and close my eyes, trying to make it all go away.

I played nice this time, and after a few days they moved me back into the more relaxed section. I continued to play by their rules, and they kept me there for six weeks.

When I was released back to my parents, I met up with some friends and got high the very first night, falling right back into my old ways. I guess the detox idea of "scared straight" actually did the opposite, because getting high and drinking became the easiest way to block out the horrific images of the drooling mental patients. It also distracted me from the anger I felt for being put in a hospital against my will.

Since my detox detour had put me out of business for more than a month, I was hurting financially. So I returned to the old reliable: stealing from my parents. My methods escalated beyond ransacking their wallets. This time I actually stole their ATM cards and started draining their accounts, taking the maximum $300 a day. Then I'd find their bank statements in the mail and rip them up before my parents could ever see them. I knew it couldn't last forever, but I got away with it for two months—way longer than I'd expected.

Eventually, their checks started bouncing. The bank called them and told them the bad news: their accounts were empty. My parents questioned me, and I fervently denied knowing anything about it, of course. I think they wanted to believe me, at least, until the bank manager showed them photos of me withdrawing money from the ATM. To make matters worse, I'd also defaulted on a bank loan Dad cosigned to help me buy a car, and the bank was trying to force him to pay off the remaining $1,200. In all, I took between $10,000 and $20,000 from my parents in a matter of months.

They were devastated. Dejected. They'd been robbed blind by their own son, their own flesh and blood. As I watched the range of emotions hit them—sadness, anger, why? why? why?—I felt my protective shell melting away. I'd been so focused on making my life momentarily better that I was ruining theirs. The realization made me want to kill myself.

Instead, I turned to the old tried-and-true combination: marijuana, cocaine, and alcohol. It was probably more cowardly than killing myself. Night after night, I was holed up in my room using until dawn, sleeping through the alarm in the morning, and skipping school for days. My parents, for the umpteenth time in their lives, were at a loss. Four months after checking me into the first hospital, they sent me to a second center for treatment.

This one was at least an improvement from the last. Here, the treatment was centered on addiction, rather than mental illness, and I was immersed in group therapy based on the Alcoholics Anonymous model. I lived within a locked ward again but was relieved to be able to have conversations with the people around me who didn't scare me like the wet brains had.

About two weeks into my four-week stay my parents paid a visit. Even as they entered the facility I could see from their faces that they weren't here because they missed me.

Nope. They'd found out that I'd introduced my younger brothers to drugs. Actually, it was more than an introduction. The three of us had all been getting high together pretty regularly. And it didn't stop there. I'd also gotten Eric to sell drugs at his school. He was eleven years old.

"You're a danger to your younger siblings," my father said to me, shaking his head. The disappointment in his voice stung.

He handed me $300. I looked up at him, mystified.

"This is your stake in the world," he said. "Make the best of it."

I was no longer welcome in their home, they made that clear. My college dreams were squashed. I'd just recently been accepted to the University of New Hampshire, but suddenly that seemed useless. My future seemed to be shriveling up right before my eyes.

I felt so guilty for luring my brothers into my upside-down world that I didn't even bother to argue. I was frightened and shocked, but I accepted my fate without question. I deserved it.

I got through the last two weeks at the rehab center fine, and then I managed to find a cheap rooming house near the hospital. When I got there, I wasn't sure what to do with myself. I knew I should get a job, but I wasn't sure where to begin looking. So I did what I'd always done. I blew the $300 my dad gave me right away, on food and beer, and once that was gone, I started stealing food. I knew it wasn't the kind of lifestyle I could sustain, but I guess deep down, I figured my parents were bluffing. Of course they'd take me back, right? I was their oldest son, after all. This was just some kind of test to show they meant business. That's what I told myself, anyway.

What I didn't realize was that in the time I was gone, Mom and Dad had taken classes on Tough Love. There, they'd learned that if they let me come home they'd just be enabling me, and we'd be right back at the same place we'd returned to year after year after year. They explained this to me and then they promptly proceeded to check me into a halfway house. I wasn't happy with the idea, but I had no choice.

◆

The place smelled. It was an old house, but I suspected its age didn't account for the odor. That came from the residents.

They were old too. I was the youngest by at least twenty-five years, and that didn't really sit well with any of us. Aside from George, the middle-aged, retired lawyer who ran the place, I couldn't manage to get along with anyone in there. Maybe it was my age. Maybe it was because I'm Jewish. Could have been my attitude, because I sure as hell didn't want to be there. Whatever the real reason, I got the feeling they looked down on me like I was some spoiled rich kid who hadn't lived through enough life to be living there. In hindsight, they were probably right.

I tried to just lay low, stay sober, and attend the recovery meetings that were part of my requirement for living there, but even I knew I was just going through the motions. Just like in the past, I still wasn't ready to be sober. This was my dad's choice, not mine, and until I made the decision to succeed, I was just going to keep failing.

After living there a month, I managed to get myself thrown out. I still don't know exactly what happened, other than I got into a fight with one of the other residents. It was lunchtime and I had made a sandwich with bacon. Some guy claimed that I didn't clean up after myself, and that was enough of an infraction for them to kick me out.

So what did I do next? You guessed it. I begged my parents to let me move back in, and this time it worked. They'd toughened, but not that much.

"I've been straight for a month," I told them, and they knew that was a pretty big deal for me. They also knew that if they said no, it could lead me down a path they didn't want to think about. They agreed to take me in, but demanded that I stay clean, get a job, and pay them rent. I agreed to their conditions and kind of stumbled along from there.

I started working as a cab driver for Holden's Taxi. It wasn't rocket science. All you had to do was get there by seven o'clock in the morning, early enough to snag a car, and then hit the road. The fares were a 60/40 split: I kept 40 percent, plus tips, and the cab company paid for all the gas and expenses. That meant cash in hand, every day. Many days I went to work flat broke and by the end of the day I had a pocket full of dough. Sure, there were light days, but I could always count on leaving with more than I had when I showed up.

Plus, the work was straightforward: you drove a car. As long as you knew the streets, and the difference between the gas and the brake, there was little thought or stress that went into the job. It was an addict's dream job. No matter what you did, you couldn't get fired. Don't show up for weeks on end? No problem. Smash the cab? No problem. Come late? You might not have a cab to drive that day, but no sweat; just come back tomorrow. Keep fares a secret? No problem. Smoking pot in the cab? Just don't get caught. Selling drugs out of the cab? Just don't get caught.

I knew all this because I tested each and every one of those things, and I never got fired. Not even for running my drug-dealing side gig out of the cab. I mean I was making as much money from selling drugs as I did off fares and tips. At my feet I kept the marijuana hidden in a trick oilcan that had a hollow bottom in which to store my stash. I was also selling coke, but I tried to limit how much I sold. It was twisted logic, but I figured the more coke I had on hand to sell, the more coke I myself would use. Even in my worst moments of depravity I knew how bad the stuff was for me—if not physically, then financially. So I restricted myself to selling it only on the weekends.

With pot, on the other hand, there was only so much I could smoke. The odds were better that even after my own take, I'd still have some left over to sell, which meant I'd have money to buy more. So I sold as much pot as I could. It wasn't hard to do. Just like when I was selling it in school, once the right customers find you, the drugs sell themselves.

Yeah, this was the job for me.

CHAPTER 4

I WAS BACK TO flying under my parents' radar. As far as they were concerned, I was sober, working, and paying rent. Only two of those three were accurate, but I let them believe what they wanted to believe. My secret hope was that if I played nice, they would change their minds and help me pay for college. I'd deferred enrollment at the University of New Hampshire when they cut me off a few months earlier. Now I was hoping I could turn things around.

As luck would have it, within a few weeks my mom and dad told me that if I kept up the good work I could enroll the next year. That was just the motivation I needed. College had always been my dream, and now it seemed close to becoming a reality. I had been acting like a loser for years, but deep down I always knew I would be a success. Maybe that's why I never worried too much about screwing up. Coming from a family of educated people, I viewed it as a given that college was the path to finding that success.

As my first semester approached, I started to think of it as an opportunity to reinvent myself. I wanted to start school with a clean slate, on equal footing with the other students. I was actually getting sick of hiding the drugs and drinking and deviance from my parents. I wanted, finally, to be the kid I told my parents I was, to become the portrait I'd painted of myself. For the first time in my life, I was ready to clean up my act.

I hit the gym and started sweating out the years and years of toxins my body had been accumulating. It was a challenge at first—dizzying, nauseating at times. But I went at it with the same kind of near obsessive perseverance I'd had with drugs and alcohol. I was so busy with getting in shape that, by default, I hardly had any time to devote to my old habits. I slimmed down, bulked up, and by the time I began classes in the fall, I had a more positive attitude than I could remember ever having had before.

The reinvention didn't stop when the summer ended. At college I continued camouflaging myself as though I was a regular college student who drank only at parties on the weekends. When you tell yourself that you're this or that for long enough, eventually you actually do become this or that, and as far as any of my fellow students knew, I had never been anything other than a social drinker. Even though the dorms would have been the perfect environment in which to sell drugs, I resisted. Now when I stayed up all night, it was because I was studying, not because I was using.

That semester was the first time I'd really fought for anything in my life, and it felt great. The buzz of confidence may not have been quite as good as coke, but it sure wasn't bad. That feeling was magnified when I learned that all my hard work had paid off: I ended the semester with a 3.89 grade point average, and I had made the dean's list.

I went home, chest puffed with pride, and delivered the news to my dad. This was the moment I had been waiting for my whole life. I had set a goal and accomplished it, plowing through obstacles and doubt. I just knew that my father would be impressed.

His response?

"Okay. Let's see if you can do it again."

I could understand his response, somewhat, considering my previous track record, but . . . it sapped every ounce of resolve out of me. It was like I was back in Cape Cod, a fat kid being forced to drink all that milk again. In my mind I'd come so far, fought so hard. And in that moment, it all disappeared.

The old cravings I'd staved off began pulsating, swirling, bubbling to the surface. He was disappointed in me when I screwed up, and he didn't act much different when I actually applied myself and accomplished something. If I couldn't even impress my own father, what good was I? What was the point of any of this?

Screw it all, I thought. *It's time to party.*

It was Christmas break, and all of my old friends from high school were home. My old habits were placed on a silver platter, right under my nose.

It was easier than ever. Johnny's mom had just moved in with her boyfriend, so he had the whole house to himself. I pretty much moved in with him and started making up for lost time.

I knew that I had one remaining $10,000 stock certificate from my grandfather. It was supposed to cover my tuition for the next semester, and I had every intention of saving the bulk of it. But once I started buying drugs, my priorities shifted. My intention to clean myself up and head back to school for the second semester disappeared somewhere in a pile of cocaine.

When the holiday break ended, I returned to campus, but my bill went unpaid. It didn't take long before I was called to the administrator's office. Sitting there, confronted, the salesman in me kicked in and I started reasoning with the administrator, explaining that I was working on getting a job to pay for tuition and I'd get it to him ASAP. He didn't seem convinced. He told me I could stay in school, but until I settled up, I wouldn't be allowed to take my final exams, and none of my records would be released.

Through it all, my father's words kept playing over and over in my head.

"Okay. Let's see if you can do it again."

I replaced my formerly good study habits with all-night benders. I'd stay up late enough to hit the cafeteria for breakfast and then muddle through classes and sleep the rest of the day. Not long thereafter I stopped going to class altogether. Hell, it wasn't like I was paying for them, after all. College was my one dream in life, and as far as I was concerned, that opportunity was gone. I figured that my life was an hourglass, and it was only a matter of time before my parents found out how badly I had screwed up. I might as well just get wasted while I was waiting for the sand to run out.

When the school finally called them, my parents were livid. After all we'd been through, they thought I was really turning my life around. They couldn't believe I'd gone from being on the dean's list back to being a degenerate. This time they took it personally. They told me this was the last straw, and I better not come crying to them. To prove their point, they converted my old bedroom into a den.

Hurt, but not surprised, I pondered my options. I was about to be out on the streets. There was really no getting around it, unless I could find a job.

I picked up a newspaper and turned to the classifieds. As I scanned the tiny print, this ad caught my eye:

Ten sharp young people wanted to travel the country
doing sales work; all living expenses provided;
no experience required!

It was like they had read my mind. This was exactly what I needed. Not only would I be making money, all of my expenses would be covered, and I would get to travel. Aside from my trips to Peru and Miami and my brief college stint, my entire life had been spent within Massachusetts.

I scheduled an interview and went in to learn more about the job. They told me that if they hired me I'd be traveling around America selling magazine subscriptions. It sounded almost luxurious—hotels, new friends, and adventure. To quell any concerns, they told me that if things didn't work out and I was unhappy, they'd buy me a bus ticket home. They made it sound as though I had nothing to lose. And from where I sat, they were right.

Well, I aced the interview and signed on immediately. I didn't bother telling them about my previous experience—the fact that by the time I had turned eighteen, I'd been in sales for more than five years. I figured the job would be a snap.

Then reality set in, beginning in Worcester, Massachusetts. The day started at 7:00 a.m. A group of students, all about my age, met in the lobby and grabbed breakfast. The manager told us we were each faced with the challenge of selling seven subscriptions a day. If we did it, we'd get paid. If we didn't, we'd have to endure a long sales meeting that lasted well into the night.

Then the manager gave us each a list of streets to hit, told us the time he'd be back to pick us up, and left us on our own. From there came a whole lot of pounding—pounding pavement, pounding doors, pounding my own dignity. The day was full of cold calls and rejection. People slammed doors in my face, yippy dogs nipped at my feet, and at one house some kid yelled to his mom, "There's some fat white guy at the door!"

After I'd taken about all the two-letter words I could handle for the day—"No," "No," "No," ad nauseam—it was time for the manager to come and pick us up. The slob was late because he'd overslept from his afternoon nap.

The days all blurred together. I tried to remain positive, because that's what you have to do in sales. I walked up to each and every door with a smile on my face, and I lied, straight through my pearly whites. "Hello (Sir or Ma'am). My name is Jay, and I am talking to people in this neighborhood about trying to raise money for our school so that we can take a trip. Would you like to help me out by buying a subscription to your favorite magazine?"

It wasn't the lies that bothered me. I was a former drug addict with a penchant for lying and stealing, remember? What bothered me was the pressure to make money. We were working on pure commission, and received a daily cash draw, which could be as low as $7 or $8 if our sales weren't up to snuff. This was the only money we'd get to buy our food and cover our expenses. The rest would be held in an account that went to pay for our nightly hotel charges. To save money, we stayed four to a room, two to a bed, and worked seven days a week. Occasionally we would have Sunday off, but only when we weren't en route to another city.

From the get-go, I got the feeling it was a racket. Our bosses maintained constant, strict control over us, feeding us information on a "need-to-know" basis and restricting us from the outside world as much as possible. But it wasn't just the leaders I didn't trust—it was my own fellow salespeople. The very first week on the job, I went to bed and placed the small amount of money I'd earned that day on the nightstand, along with the money I'd brought with me. When I awoke, it was gone. That was the last bit of money I had to my name. Without it, I knew, I was really stuck here.

We made our way to Warwick, Rhode Island, and then to Virginia Beach, Virginia. As I got deeper and deeper into it, I came to grips with the fact that when it came to selling legal products, I pretty much sucked.

I didn't get any better with time, and my manager started getting frustrated. He decided maybe subscriptions weren't the best match for my skill set. The magazine company had a sister company that sold cleaning fluid. Not just any cleaning fluid, of course, but some super-duper cleaner that you could buy only by the gallon, and for a ridiculous price (409 was cheaper and just as effective).

I decided to try my hand at that, see if I could do any better. The sales spiel on that particular route was actually more in-depth than the magazine script. I didn't just knock on doors: I convinced people to let me into their homes so I could give them a demonstration. It was more of a marathon pitch than a sprint pitch. The company saw this as a plus for me, because it would give me more time to really work the sale and convince the buyer that he or she simply could not live without this product.

I dutifully went door-to-door, up and down the East Coast, trying to hawk that "miracle" cleaner. Well. I was terrible at that too.

The one good thing that came from this job was the fact that I stayed pretty clean the whole time I was out there. The honest truth was I couldn't afford do otherwise. With an average draw of $10 to $15 a day, I had to put eating ahead of drinking and drugs. On the rare times when we would get a Saturday night or a Sunday off, a few of us pooled our cash, made a liquor store run, and got drunk in one of our rooms. Woo hoo! It wasn't much of an existence.

We began traveling west. By this time I'd been with the company nearly six months and had pretty well solidified my reputation as a subpar salesman. After investing so much time in me, my bosses were getting pretty sick of my results. The whole way out to Oklahoma they'd been nagging me about it, sending me to "attitude adjustment" meetings, which only made the bitterness grow. The more they insulted me, the angrier I got. It took me back to my childhood, and I felt like my dad was berating me all over again while I hid behind my spaghetti. I hated feeling that way. I was an adult now and vowed not to let anyone make me feel that way ever again. I quit. I told them I wasn't taking it anymore.

"I'm ready for that bus ticket home," I said to my manager. "The one you promised when I signed up."

As soon the words left my mouth, he growled something about how he'd send my sorry ass back to Massachusetts, but I'd have to wait "until arrangements could be made." That meant until he found a cheap ticket.

When one person leaves this kind of organization, it's only natural for others to follow. My manager wanted to guard against that possibility, so he quarantined me, locking me in a room of my own so I didn't "contaminate" the others. I waited, sleeping, pacing, watching TV, and craving a freaking drink. Finally, the manager and another guy came and got me and took me to the bus station.

♦

It was a three-day ride, with connections from Oklahoma City back to Boston. I mostly kept to myself on the bus, looking out the window and catching up on some sleep. During the stops I took advantage of the free water fountains and tried not to think about food. I literally had no money to my name, not even enough for a burger.

By the second day, the hunger pangs were fighting for some TLC. They started slow, just a tickle here and there, but before long I couldn't concentrate. I'd made it a habit not to feel hunger pangs most of my life. As a consequence, when they hit, they really floored me.

Painful as it was, that hunger got me to thinking. I'd had it pretty easy up to now. Sure, I had a rough home life and had gotten into some heavy stuff. In terms of food, water, shelter, and all the basics, though, I'd always had those, and I'd always taken them for granted. It wasn't until I was deprived of all that, for the very first time, that I realized how essential that handful of things was. Most of us are so wrapped up in our daily problems, our personal dramas and stresses, that we never sit back and think about the important things and how lucky we are to have them. Surrounded by strangers, trapped in these strange thoughts, I felt hopelessly alone.

We stopped at Grand Central Station in New York City late that night. I was getting closer to home, but it was a weird feeling. I knew that when I got to Boston I had no idea where my actual home would be.

My connecting bus wasn't leaving until the next morning, which gave me hours and hours to ponder my hunger. It had now been two full days since I'd eaten anything, and I was determined to find something before the morning.

In the past I would have gone into a store and stolen something. But it was late, and my options were limited. My eyes scanned the station and came to rest on what looked like a half-eaten donut near a pay phone. I walked up to it, looked over my shoulder to the left and over my shoulder to the right. Satisfied that no one was looking, I scarfed down the donut. The sweet, fried treat was delicious, but it was a tease, not nearly enough to even take the edge off my ravenous hunger. I licked the sugar off my fingers and wished for more.

Looking around again, I took in my surroundings . . . bench, ashtray, newspaper, pay phone. Pay phone! I walked over and checked the coin return for stray nickels and dimes. Nothing. I kept searching, and the neighboring phones were better: 85 cents better, to be exact. It was enough to buy another donut and make a phone call once I got to Boston. I still wasn't sure how I'd find a ride from the station.

I had the rest of the night to just sit. I dozed a little, but mostly I observed the characters around me. There was a bag lady wandering about, rummaging around in the trashcans. A scraggly homeless man in a worn green sports jacket slept on a bench. I could see straight through the holes in his shoes to his feet. As I watched these two indigents, I tried not to think about how similar the three of us were. Eventually, a cop shooed them off. I stuck around until my bus came, and four hours after that I was back in Boston, where I had no job, no job prospects, and little more than a family that had clearly disowned me.

CHAPTER 5

I USED THE CHANGE I found to call Mitch. He picked me up and drove me straight to the liquor store to buy a couple of quarts of beer. Between that and a joint, my hunger was staved off for the time being. It was the best homecoming I could have asked for.

Mitch took me over to Johnny's house, and he said I could stay there again. It was just like old times. We drank and did coke at night, and during the day I worked at a pretty mindless job doing landscaping. For a few weeks, it worked out fine. But I could tell I was getting on Johnny's nerves. From his comments, I got the sense that he thought I was sponging off him. And in truth, I was. I was eating his food, leaving dishes in his sink, drinking his liquor. I'd go down to the basement and see what he had there, and if it looked good, I drank it. How was I to know that the sweet stuff I chugged actually belonged to his uncle?

I wasn't making any effort to be "Houseguest of the Year," that's for sure. So when I borrowed his car one day without asking and disappeared for a few hours, it was the last straw. I came home to a seething Johnny. "You stole my car!" he accused me. Then he kicked me out.

That same day I lost my landscaping job. They actually expected their employees to show up on time for work and do their job well. I did neither, so they fired me.

I went right back to where I always went. I tucked my tail between my legs, checked my pride at the door, and begged my parents to give me a place to stay. They listed the same conditions as always: I had to stay off drugs and alcohol, work, and pay rent. When I agreed to that, they reluctantly agreed to take me in. I slept in the basement on a mattress by the pool table.

As much as my parents wanted to play tough, the bottom line was their kid needed help. I think that in some ways they felt responsible for my struggles. They created me, after all. But aside from giving me shelter and ground rules, they didn't have the slightest clue about what to do with me.

I went back to driving a taxi and doing some drug sales on the side, and soon I was making enough money to afford my own place. I moved out from under the watchful eyes of my parents and began indulging my habits even more freely.

I developed a routine. Smoke, sell drugs, and drive all day. Then at night I would have a pocket full of cash to spend at the Backyard, my regular bar. It was a short bus ride from there to the room I was renting, so after I was done drinking at the bar, I would hop on a bus with a six-pack and head home. I was twenty years old now, still underage, but I had a couple of IDs at my disposal. The first was my true driver's license, which I had altered pretty easily by scraping off the lamination and typing a different birthday. I also bought a fake one for backup.

My drink of choice was usually a screwdriver or beer. Occasionally, I'd drink whiskey and ginger ale, just like the old man. Whatever the drink, once I started I was in for the long haul. A couple of times a bartender would say I'd had enough, but was I listening? I'd stay at the bar until last call and then stumble home and pour myself another. Pour, drink, repeat; pour, drink, repeat, until I passed out. I was becoming just like my father.

It took a lot of drinks before I would pass out because, in between, I was snorting coke. That kept me alert and helped me keep going. Most nights I would have what was called a "grayout." It wasn't quite a blackout, but chunks of my memory would be missing. I'd feel like hell the next day, but I always managed to rally. I just had to make it until five or six o'clock in the evening, and then work was over and the cycle could begin again.

Through it all I forced myself to be responsible for two things: I always made sure I saved enough money for rent and had cash to pay my dealer. Outside of that, anything I had was as good as gone.

◆

Not surprisingly, I was starting to lose touch with reality. Now that I was living on my own, I did what I wanted when I wanted to, and for the life of me, I couldn't even get fired from my job. I was starting to think I was invincible. Then the run-ins with the law began.

It was a Thursday night, and we started out in an area known as the "Combat Zone." It was a seedy part of Boston known for its strip clubs, X-rated bookstores, adult movie theaters, massage parlors, and prostitutes. Johnny and I were hanging out—once I moved out of his house we quickly became friends again—and we ended up at a strip club there, getting drunk on Long Island iced teas, a drink that's got all the white liquors (gin, rum, vodka, tequila, and a little bit of triple sec), sweet-and-sour mix, and cola.

After a few hours there we decided to visit a second strip club, where we continued drinking Long Island iced teas while admiring the entertainment. By the time we left, we'd both been drinking for nearly six hours and were pretty smashed. We climbed into Johnny's car, and right away he ran a red light. By the time he stopped at the next traffic signal, flashing lights and sirens surrounded us. We were screwed.

The cops motioned for us to get out of the car. I opened the door, stood up, and before I could even open my mouth—WHAM! I saw stars. It felt like I'd hit my head on something, and it turned out I had—the cop's fist. He hit me straight on, and I could feel my head swelling instantly. As I got my bearings, I saw another cop waving around a plastic bag that had three smaller bags of marijuana in it. My stomach dropped—that was my stash.

I was cuffed and thrown in the back of a police car. As we pulled away, I watched Johnny climb back in his car after they let him go. I don't know why or how, but they didn't seem to notice his drunkenness. Maybe it was because I was plastered, but none of it made much sense: How did they know I had pot on me? Was I really going to jail? What the . . . I was pretty scared.

The cops drove me to the police station, fingerprinted me, and told me that I was being charged with possession of marijuana with intent to distribute. Then they threw me in a cell. By then the liquor was starting to wear off, and I was starting to get just how serious the situation was. I was in some pretty dire straits.

I sat awake all night in my dreary, depressing cell, surrounded by the screams of other inmates. It was like they all knew each other and were talking like neighbors in an apartment complex. Getting arrested must have been a regular thing for a lot of those guys. I told myself that I never wanted to be like them. But at the same time, it made me feel even more alone.

My cell was tiny, and it felt smaller with every hour that passed. There was nothing to do but sit and try not to think about the smell of urine and crap from the toilet. The thought of suicide actually crossed my mind. Not seriously, because I knew my time in the cell would be limited. But it made sense to me why someone in this situation would do it. It would be a way of regaining control. Right then, I was no better off than a caged animal.

Johnny got there Friday morning, along with my friend George (who was into sales, like me), and my younger brother Eric, and they bailed me out. What a relief. If it weren't for them, I would have been transferred from my holding cell over to the county jail to await trial. One night in a cell by myself was bad enough. Who knows what would have happened at County.

I was dying for a drink and just about anything else that would dull the pain of what I'd been through. On top of feeling all-out dejected, the bruises on my face from the cop's fist were really smarting. Johnny expected I'd feel that way, so he already had plans to drive us over to a dank apartment in a seedy part of the South End of Boston (actually, most of the South End was pretty seedy those days), where we freebased cocaine until the wee hours of the morning.

Monday morning I needed to calm my nerves before my arraignment, so I got high before going to court. I was completely unfamiliar with the legal system, so I had no idea what I was in for. I arrived at the courthouse around eight o'clock and listened as they called name after name and read charge after charge. Two hours there felt like an eternity. Finally, I heard "Jay Littmann." Then they read my charges: possession of marijuana with the intent to distribute.

"Do you have a lawyer?" the judge asked. I told him I didn't, so he appointed a public defender to represent me and allowed me to stay out on bail.

The public defender was an older guy with gray hair encircling the bottom of his head. "Inept" was the first word that came to mind when we shook hands. Looking him up and down, I struggled to face the fact that my fate lay in the hands of an attorney who dressed in a suit straight out of Goodwill.

He had a game plan mapped out, however, and said that I could probably plead no contest to possession, which is a misdemeanor, and the district attorney would drop the intent to distribute part. He went on to explain that when you pleaded no contest to possession of marijuana in the state of Massachusetts, and it was your first offense, it would be dismissed after six months, leaving no record.

It sounded like a get-out-of-jail-free card to me. I agreed, already feeling relieved. With the next court date a month away, I made it my mission to not give it too much more thought.

Around that time, the house where I'd been renting a room was sold, and so I asked my parents if I could move back in with them. Begrudgingly they agreed, and I returned to the same old, same old right up to my appointed court day. And I mean right up to it.

My court date was on a Friday, and I woke up early, dreadfully hung over. I was nervous. If everything didn't go as planned I knew I'd be pissed if I had to trade partying that weekend for a jail cell.

Everything went even better than my lawyer predicted. One of the arresting officers showed up to testify, and he brought along the marijuana they'd taken from me. I still don't know how or why, but he held it in such a way that it looked like it was one bag rather three. That, in the court of law, is a huge difference. Three bags meant you were selling; one, you were just using. So, in the end, I got little more than a slap on the wrist. If I could manage to just stay out of trouble for six months, they would drop the charges.

Time to celebrate.

My parents were out of town, so the very next night I borrowed my mom's Chrysler station wagon. After enjoying quite a few mai tais at a Chinese restaurant, I started getting a yen for cocaine. Generally, that meant I was drunk and needed a sobering pick-me-up in the form of expensive white powder. I called a dealer I knew who lived in Quincy, just about half an hour from Boston, and stumbled to my car.

I almost made it. As I was trying to find his house, I noticed a police car behind me. I got nervous and turned the corner, hoping to shake it. When the lights started flashing, I panicked, slamming my foot on the gas like it was some kind of chase scene out of "Starsky and Hutch." The tires squealed as I tore through side streets. Every time I thought I'd made ground I caught sight of the squad car's flashing lights in my rearview.

The chase went on for what seemed an eternity. It must have been nearly twenty minutes before I realized that the cops weren't going to disappear. In a last-ditch effort, I pulled the car into someone's driveway, got out, and ran. With the adrenalin running through my alcohol-slogged veins, I managed to keep up a decent pace and even jumped a few fences. I was no Bruce Jenner, but for an overweight drunk I managed pretty well. After hightailing it through a few backyards, I hid behind someone's shed.

Crouched down, I felt my heart race and heard my jagged breathing. I was panicking over what might come next—a DUI? Worse? Time stood completely still. Next thing I knew, some guy came walking right through that backyard toward me. His voice was kind, concerned.

"Do you need some help or something?" he asked.

"No, I'm okay," I told him. Then he said he was a detective with the police force, and he needed me to go with him.

A whole pack of police cars had gathered by now, and all their lights were flashing as we walked toward them. Out of the corner of my eye I saw that a tow truck had come for my mom's station wagon.

They cuffed me, read me my rights, and threw me into the back of the cruiser. Then they asked me if I wanted a Breathalyzer or a blood test. The law said they had to offer both.

"Blood test," I said without hesitation. Even in my drunkenness I knew it would be a challenge for them, because it took more time and expertise than a Breathalyzer did, and that would give me time to sober up.

I overheard one of the cops saying they would have to take me to the hospital in order to perform the test, and they didn't want to deal with the hassle. Well, thank God for that because it meant they weren't going to bother charging me with drunken driving. They did, however, take the time to search my mom's car, and they found a roach (meaning the stub of a marijuana cigarette), which gave them reason to charge me with possession of marijuana and failing to stop for the police.

Back to jail. The Quincy cells weren't as bad as the ones in Boston; well, at least they didn't stink so much. The worst part was being alone with my thoughts again. They weren't pretty, those thoughts, and they hit me like a freight train. Just twenty-four hours earlier I'd felt like I'd won, beaten the system, accomplished something. Now that was replaced by an even more profound low. How could I have been so stupid as to get myself into this situation again? Why did I do this to myself? Why did I feel this bad? Why did I live this way? Why couldn't I just stop doing this to myself? I prayed to God, telling Him that if He'd just help me get out of this, I'd straighten up. I'd really do it this time.

The next morning George bailed me out. He took me back to my parents' house, and luckily they were still out of town. My sister Barbara was home, though, and she immediately noticed that the car was gone. She had planned on using it that day. She took one look at me and started to cry. She could tell I screwed up.

As the youngest, Barbara was always the good kid of the family, and she had to put up with a lot. I was always doing things like this, putting her in a tough spot. Mostly, she was upset because she didn't know whether to lie or tell the truth to my parents. If she ratted me out, they would kick me out of the house for sure, and that would weigh heavy on her shoulders. If she didn't, it would be just another lie to add to an already long list.

I didn't know what to say to her, so I didn't say anything at all.

The judge allowed me to stay out on bail. This time, I wanted to avoid dealing with an incompetent public defender, so I hired an attorney, who was referred to me by one of my customers. I quickly learned a lesson: Never trust the referral of a druggie. The lawyer didn't even bother showing up in court after the first appearance, so I ended up working out a deal myself, with the assistant district attorney. It was the same deal as I'd just made in Boston: no contest to possession of marijuana as my first offense. Just like before, it would be dismissed after six months, leaving no record.

Because the court systems weren't linked in any way, what happened in Boston was a mystery in Quincy, and vice versa. The different districts pretty much kept to themselves, and I was able to get off with two identical first offenses. I didn't know if some kind of higher power was looking after me, or if it was just dumb luck. Either way, I was grateful for it—just not grateful enough to change my ways.

◆

When my old pal Franx asked if I wanted to get a place together, I jumped at the chance to move out of my folks' house. He'd found a one-bedroom apartment in the Fenway part of Boston. We divided it up—I took the bedroom and he took the living room.

The Fenway neighborhood is central to more than just the famous Fenway Park. Our apartment sat in a hub of activity, surrounded by bars. We had some friends that were in a punk rock band that played near our place, so the apartment became the go-to spot for parties.

Being around the late-night music scene meant I was around cocaine a lot more, and I started using it every day. It was a vicious cycle. The more I used, the more I needed to sell to be able to support my habit. I needed cash.

In hopes of making more money, I started attending a school that trained people to become real estate agents. The training lasted about three months, and I passed with flying colors. But when it came time to actually make a sale, I might as well have been peddling magazines and cleaning fluid.

It probably didn't help that I'd met a dealer who lived right in my building, so I was pretty much high all the time. He became my go-to guy, always there when I needed him. Well, almost always.

One night Franx and I were having a party, and we were all drinking and getting pretty wasted. I suggested we get some coke to help us all sober up. Everyone agreed, so I called my dealer, but he wasn't answering the phone. I walked over to his apartment and saw that the lights were on, and I heard music playing. I knocked on his door, but for some reason he wasn't answering. *Knock knock knock.* No answer. The louder I knocked the more frustrated I felt. When a guy needs to get high, a guy needs to get high, and I didn't like the fact that he was leaving me in the lurch. I was convinced that he was just sleeping in there, and I knew deep down in my heart that he wouldn't want to miss out on a sale like this. There was no question about it. I had to wake him up.

So I climbed the fire escape to his window. It was covered with mesh to keep people from doing just what I was doing, but I was drunk and determined. I gripped that mesh, and with all my strength, I tried to rip it right off the window.

That's when I looked close, real close, inside and saw a look of terror I will never forget. A little girl was crouching below the window. She was maybe eight or nine years old, and her eyes were wide, horrified. Her mother and father were next to her, their eyes, too, wide with fear.

I was at the wrong apartment.

Freaked out myself, I climbed back down the fire escape and returned to the party. I was amped on adrenalin and shock. I sat down and tried to chill out. Just as my heart rate was returning to normal, someone knocked on the door.

It was a whole fleet of police. The family had seen me return to my apartment and called the cops, but since there was a party going on, the cops weren't sure who they were looking for.

"If the person who tried to break in next door doesn't come forward then we'll be taking everyone down to the station for questioning!" one of the cops yelled.

He was met with silence, which grew more uncomfortable with each passing second. My mind reeled. I knew that I was facing a breaking-and-entering charge, and evading that could only hurt me worse. This was serious and could net me real prison time.

"It was me," I fessed up. They cuffed me, walked me downstairs, and put me in the back of the cop car. The rest of the night went by in a blur. I was still plastered, and picked up only bits and pieces, like the screaming going on around me, and the endless talking. Lots and lots of talking. I must have passed out somewhere in there.

The next morning Johnny was there, bailing me out. He brought along three members of the band, and they took me back to the apartment. Franx was waiting for us, and it didn't look good.

Things with Franx had been tense for a while. The typical roommate stuff—dirty dishes, taking food, that kind of stuff—had been driving him crazy. But add to that all the drugs and drinking we were doing, and the tension skyrocketed.

Now I'd screwed things up at his home, and screwed them up pretty badly. He was so upset about what I'd done that he couldn't even get the words out. So he just up and hit me, punched me in the face. I stumbled to get my footing, and next thing I knew we were all-out wrestling. He was grabbing my head and I was doing my best to defend myself. I don't think either of us knew what was up and what was down, we were just seeing red. We'd both gotten in a few punches when the four other guys pried us apart and broke it up.

As I left with them I could hear Franx hollering out the window, "Don't come back here!"

Johnny, the musicians, and I went to breakfast like nothing had happened.

♦

Before my hearing I was determined to see what kind of magic I could work to save myself from becoming a felon. It turned out I knew the man who lived in the apartment I'd tried to get into. He was an immigrant from Haiti, and I'd actually helped him out once when his car was dead and needed a jump start. So I paid him a visit. I told him that it was all a big accident. I had been drunk and out of my mind, I said, and I apologized.

He recognized me from the time I had helped him, and he accepted my apology. I convinced him to come to court and tell the judge that it was an accident and that he didn't want the charges to stick.

It worked. All the charges were dismissed. My third get-out-of-jail free card was even easier to come by than the earlier ones. It was some luck I had on my side.

But the problems were just starting on the home front. Franx was still irate, so he moved out of the apartment. I couldn't afford to live there on my own, so the most logical thing to do, in my mind, was to just stop paying rent. I knew that the Massachusetts landlord-tenant laws favored the tenant, and I also happened to know that it was an arduous process to get someone evicted. In other words, I acted like a real jerk and continued ignoring the eviction notices that my landlord posted on the front door. I remained there as a squatter while he went through the standard procedures to get me out. I became a bum in my own home.

With no rent to pay, and no bills to pay once the power was shut off, I started missing more and more work. Cab driving may be easy, but it wasn't as easy as drinking, smoking pot, and being a slug on the couch. The more drugs I did, the worse the apartment got. The trash just piled up for weeks on end and became a breeding ground for insects. Cockroaches roamed the apartment, skittering around rotting chicken and other food scraps I hadn't gotten around to cleaning. It wasn't a pretty sight.

Even in the depths of my depravity I knew I couldn't go on like this forever. At some point, the eviction was going to come through and I'd need a place to go. So I started working on my parents, and they agreed to take me back in. They offered to help me move, and brought my brother, Eric, over to the apartment to pick up my stuff. They could barely get past the stench, the smell of death that permeated the place. All three were in utter disbelief that I could live like that. Seeing their reactions, I was pretty embarrassed—that is, in the few moments when I was sober enough to know the difference.

I'd added freebasing to my list of illicit hobbies around that time. It was extremely addictive and put me in a state where I barely had the mental capacity—or energy—to do anything else. I was so far gone and reckless that it wasn't much of a surprise when I came back to my parents' home one day to find that my stash of drugs to sell weren't in their normal hiding place. My father had found them. Again.

"I'll move out," I pleaded with him, "but I need my drugs. All of my money is tied up in them."

He threatened to call the cops on me. I just kept hammering away, telling him that without those drugs to sell I'd be forced to go live on the streets. He wasn't budging, so I got desperate and started yelling at him. I was a little over six feet one and 300 pounds at that time, but I don't know that my size intimidated him at all.

"Those drugs are all I have in the whole world!"

There I was, reduced to begging, screaming. I was pathetic, and we both knew it. In the end, I think he took pity on me. He gave the drugs back, and I left, but I had no place to go.

CHAPTER 6

I DROVE TO UPSTATE New York to visit my friend George. He'd been staying at his grandfather's cabin since the old man had passed away and had the whole place to himself. I figured it was as good a time as any to disappear for a while.

I remember very little about the days that followed. We went on a binge to end all binges, freebasing for five days straight. We'd sleep a few hours here and there, when we were able to, and the only time we left the cabin was to go on a run for beer or food.

Then I returned to the Boston area to find a place to live, and I ended up renting a room in an attic in Waltham, Massachusetts. You'd think I would have gotten the binging out of my system, but I stayed there for days on end just smoking cocaine. The only variation in my schedule was when I ran out of coke or when I needed to sleep. Then, I turned to the bottle.

I made self-medicating into an art form, but even I lacked the powers to avoid the downside of it all. On the bad days there was this kind of nausea at the pit of my stomach, accentuated by tobacco acid and lack of food. The worst part was always the aggravating heaviness that accumulated at the top of my forehead, reminding me I hadn't slept for days. It was like having a wet headband on the front of my head, and it wouldn't go away. But as much as I despised it, it never stopped me.

When I finally ran out of my supplies, I left the attic and returned to work as a courier. I had quit my job driving the cab because I'd heard I could make even better money doing this. Truth be told, by the time I went back after my bender, it was actually pretty amazing I still had a job. I had been gone more than a week, yet they hardly even seemed to miss me. It was probably the only position I could have found that had more freedom than the taxi gig. My route was simple: I drove a van to sorting centers where I delivered mail. The work was mindless, just as I liked it, and I put in fewer than seven hours a day, working a few days on, a few days off. It complemented my drug habits nicely.

One day I was working my route, not really paying much attention to anything. I'd been smoking pot to try and get me through a horrendous hangover. Driving along, I veered onto a semicircular street and didn't notice the truck turning from the opposite direction. Next thing I knew, this semi, loaded with metal pipes, was right in front of me, and no amount of swerving could save me.

As I smashed into the truck, the steering wheel was crushed around my hands and the interior of the van caved in around me. Crashing, screeching, crunching noises surrounded me—and then, all was still.

I looked around, taking inventory. I was still alive. I knew that much. Right in front of me I could see all the truck's metal pipes, dangerously close. There was blood on the steering wheel. My blood. I could see my wrist was all messed up and so was my hand. The rest I wasn't sure about; I just knew that my body hurt, everywhere.

Cars stopped all around me and passersby stared in at me, curious and concerned. The truck driver asked if I was okay, and he called for help. I sat there in silence, pinned in my van. Everything hurt so bad I wasn't even sure where the pain was coming from. Mostly I was worried that when the police got there they would find my hash I had stored in the cigarette pack on the dashboard.

I heard the sirens and then saw the lights as the fire trucks and ambulances arrived. There was a flurry of activity followed by the buzz of tools. I heard the sound of a loud motor, like a lawn mower, and watched as sparks flew and big metal claws grabbed the van, whizzing through it like a chainsaw. They were cutting me out with the Jaws of Life. Once they sliced open the van they carefully lifted me out and secured me on a stretcher so I couldn't move. As they took me away, my mind just kept flashing back to that hashish on the dash.

When I got to the hospital, the doctor told me I had a broken hand and wrist and a bunch of heavy bruises and sprains all over my body. I was a mess—a big, swollen, painful mess. They put both arms in slings, and I couldn't even walk without crutches. I was pretty worried about what I'd do, how I'd take care of myself. But then the doctor gave me a prescription for painkillers and the worry vanished. *Those*, I thought to myself, *will go well with a cocktail.*

Johnny picked me up at the hospital, and our first stop was the liquor store. When we got to the house, I popped some painkillers and started drinking right away. Within minutes I was dizzy, spaced out and woozy, which didn't much help with the already difficult trek up the three flights of stairs to get to my room. Reality finally set in. How would I get through this physically, much less financially?

I filed for workers' comp, and they awarded me $14,000 to cover my medical expenses and pain and suffering. It seemed like a decent chunk of change at the time, but I knew that it wouldn't last forever, and I had to figure out some way to make money. Obviously, I was in no shape to drive a van or taxi anymore. My only option seemed to be dealing drugs. But could I stay in business if I wasn't mobile? I had always avoided having my customers over to the house because I had room-mates, and I didn't want to attract a lot of attention to myself. Now, something had to give.

About two weeks after the accident, the couple that I had been rent-ing the attic from moved out. The timing couldn't have been better. I talked to the landlord and told him I wanted to rent the whole house, not just a room. I figured I could take it upon myself to sublet whatever space I needed to in order to get by and at least have a say over who I was living with, which would make it easier to sell drugs. So I put an ad in the local paper to find roommates, and I moved onto the porch—a 10-foot-by-12-foot enclosed space at the front of the house—in order to free up the attic and every other room in the house and bring in more money. The porch wasn't so bad. I had a cot to sleep on, and I bought a $40 heater. It could have been much worse.

Then I heard from an old friend of mine, Craig. Back in the day, he had been driving a cab for the rival cab company in Newton. We'd kept in touch over the years, so when he came to visit Boston and needed a place to stay, I told him I had a room to rent.

Craig was a heavy drinker too, and we both quickly learned that together the two of us were nothing but trouble. If it wasn't one thing, it was another. Like the time we stole (although I preferred to think we "borrowed") my father's boat. The two of us had been up all night drinking and smoking all kinds of stuff, and I mentioned that my dad had a boat that he stored at my parents' house. Suddenly, the only thing we knew was that we needed to be in that 8-foot-long wooden boat immediately, driving it a good fifty miles from Wareham to Martha's Vineyard through the Cape Cod Canal.

So that's just what we did. Despite the fact that we were both wrecked, we managed to get over to my parents' vacant second home and climb into the boat without waking anyone in the neighborhood. Then, we were off. It was a dangerous trip. The canal is known for its strong undercurrents, but we were so smashed we hardly even noticed. After a few hours we made it, unscathed. We looked at each other like, "What now?" and then turned her around and headed home.

That was when the undercurrents really kicked in. The combination of Mother Nature and exhaustion were too much for either of us to handle. Water started dumping in the boat, filling it so fast that it actually felt like it was about to splinter.

"We gotta beach her!" I yelled at Craig.

Just as we were heading toward shore, the Coast Guard showed up. They said they'd gotten a call from someone on a private beach and were there to tow us in. They let the two of us go, but not until after

they'd written us up for a bunch of violations, which eventually made their way back to my dad. It didn't exactly help our relationship.

A few days later, Craig and I and our other roommate, Andrew, were all sitting around, shooting the shit, waiting for a customer to come pick up a quarter-ounce of cocaine and a half-ounce of pot. I was rolling a joint in hopes of making myself feel better after a night of partying when a loud knock on the door shattered any semblance of quiet. I went to answer it.

"Get down! Get down on the floor!"

Cops. Damn. I did as I was told, and while I was doing it, one of them shoved a badge in my face and put a gun to my head and then about a dozen plainclothes cops filed into my house. They had a search warrant. I was totally helpless as they tore the place apart.

The lead police officer put Craig, Andrew, and me into separate rooms as a way of intimidating us. While I sat there, waiting, I heard a knock on the front door.

Go away, I thought, trying to communicate telepathically with whoever was behind the door. *Just go away.*

One of the cops answered it with his gun drawn.

"Come join the party," he said and pulled the guy inside. It was my customer.

The cops, who had clearly been watching me and the house, questioned each of us individually. I refused to tell them where the mother lode of my stash was, and so did Craig, but Andrew wasn't so tough. He cracked pretty quickly and said he'd seen me go down to the cellar a bunch of times. He told them he saw me use a key to open the padlock on the door down there.

So the lead cop took my key ring and quickly found the padlock key. The cops went downstairs and made a beeline for the refrigerator. I'd been getting careless about leaving the fridge door open. It took them all of about a second to find just what they were looking for: 5 pounds of pot in four different varieties, along with various vials, scales, and pipes hidden behind one of the vegetable drawers. They combined that with

the pot and coke that I had for my customer upstairs and announced that I was under arrest for possession of both marijuana and cocaine with the intent to distribute. They also threw in a charge for manufacturing cocaine, because of the vials.

The police took me and Craig away. I wasn't aware of it until then, but apparently he had an outstanding warrant on some unrelated matter, some kind of vehicle violation compounded by a failure-to-appear charge. They didn't charge Andrew, though, or my customer. I was the one they were really after.

Left alone once more in a cell, I mentally ran through the list of people I could call to help me out with bail. I hated being in this position. I was still estranged from my parents, and I had grown apart from a lot of my old friends. Those I hadn't grown apart from had bailed me out so often in the past that I couldn't bear to ask them to do it again. Besides, the bail was high this time—$10,000 high.

I ended up calling my mom's sister, Linda. I had always been close to my aunt, and I felt like she was one of the few people I could trust with my checkbook, which the police allowed her to bring so I could pay my own bail. It was basically all that was left from the workers' comp settlement, and all the money I had in the world.

Craig wasn't so lucky. They were holding him on some kind of warrant that wasn't eligible for bail until he was transported to the jurisdiction of the original complaint. There was nothing I could do for him financially, so I brought him a submarine sandwich. He didn't seem very hungry.

When I got home, I poured myself a stiff drink and then went around taking inventory to see what the cops got and what they'd missed. They hadn't found the cocaine that I kept hidden in my WD-40 oilcan, the same oilcan I had used back in my cab-driving days. I breathed a sigh of relief. At least my stash wasn't totally dried up. I removed the false bottom and partook until I was numb. *I'm going to have to be more careful from now on,* I thought to myself.

My arraignment came and went. It was a familiar process by now. I'd learned from my last experience not to trust a customer's referral, so instead I went straight to the top. I used a lawyer recommended by my own dealer.

I realized something was awry when the guy asked me to pick him up from his office and drive him to court. Apparently, he didn't even have a car. *What a winner*, I thought. *Do I really want this guy on my case?*

On the way there, he started smoking a joint so fat you could barely get your mouth around it. I mean this stuff was straight out of a Cheech and Chong movie. As he puffed away he asked if I wanted some, and I declined. I didn't want to walk into the courtroom facing drug charges reeking of pot. He, on the other hand, didn't seem bothered by the possibility. I drove the rest of the way in horror.

Even with all those red flags, I kept him on. I figured if my dealer had such high praise for him, he couldn't be all that bad. I knew he'd gotten my dealer off some serious charges in the past, and I knew from experience that engaging in recreational drug use did not make you a stupid or incompetent person. I mean, look at me. So I kept the faith.

♦

For the first time in my criminal career, the arrest got written up in the local newspaper, the *Waltham Daily News Tribune*. "Jay Littmann, a 25-year-old man, was arrested with over 5 pounds of marijuana and an ounce of cocaine plus various drug paraphernalia at his home in Waltham."

I read it over and over again. It wasn't so much the content that got me; I just kept fixating on that one little word—"man." Reading it in black and white was a real reality check. Where had my life gone?

It was a pretty low moment. It forced me to really look at myself, and who I'd become. All of my life I'd equated the word "man" with people like my father and my father's friends. Compared to them I was just some kind of lost kid, and as long as I was a lost kid, I felt like I could get away with just about anything. Now I was being called a man, and there was nothing I could do about it because it was true. It didn't matter that

I still didn't know who I was or who I wanted to be. It didn't matter that I'd thrown so much away already and that I wasn't sure if I'd be able to salvage any of it. Regardless of how much I acted like a child, I was a man and I needed to deal with it.

I caught a glimpse of myself in the mirror. I'd been up for several days, using, and it showed. My clothes were filthy, and I couldn't remember the last time I had taken a shower. Staring at that mirror I was drawn into my own gaze, trying to see what was behind it. The answer? Nothing.

It was a moment of truth. In those few seconds I knew I had lost all control over my life. I couldn't stop doing what I was doing no matter how hard I tried. Thinking about that, I couldn't stop crying. Tears turned into sobs, and for nearly four hours I was just beside myself. I was sad, helpless, and pathetic.

When I finally regained my composure, I went straight to my pipe. I sat there smoking, wishing I could cover all the mirrors in the world.

I pulled myself together enough to make it to court a number of times that month, and each time I was pleased to see that my attorney did a pretty good job. He was stoned out of his mind, but he still did good enough to get the prosecutor to offer me a deal: plead guilty to misdemeanor possession charges on both the marijuana and the cocaine and he'd recommend a suspended sentence, probation, and fines, but no jail time. I jumped at the deal. I didn't know what I did to deserve such luck, but there it was again. I never really knew it at the time, but as much as that luck felt like a blessing, it was also a curse. Every time I got off easy it gave me even less incentive to clean up my act.

After paying all those attorney's fees, I was broke, desperate, and feeling pretty low. I wasn't really sure what to do with myself. I stopped paying rent once again, but I kept collecting it from my roommates so I could afford my habits. Those habits pretty much took up all of my time. I guess I just figured things would work out like they always had. If I kept doing what I was doing I'd keep getting what I was getting. I was on autopilot.

That's when I got a surprise visit from Craig. He'd gotten out of jail a little while earlier and met a woman who lived in Hyannis, on Cape Cod. He had moved in with her and her sixteen-year-old daughter. After I told him about my own problems, he offered to set up a cot for me in the living room of their two-bedroom cottage.

At that point in my life, I'd alienated just about everyone I'd ever been close with. I had no money, no job, and no girl. I had nothing to lose, and Craig knew he didn't have to ask me twice. I grabbed my stuff and got out of Dodge, picking up a bottle of booze along the way.

CHAPTER 7

DEEDEE AND CRAIG WERE quite the pair. She was fifty-two years old, which was twenty-five years his senior, and looked as though she'd been beaten down by life. Short and stocky, DeeDee was nice enough when she was sober, but her personality changed when she drank, and she was embodied by this hungry anger that made her appear larger than life. Like Craig, she was an alcoholic, and every night the two of them drank Black Russians until either they passed out or World War III began.

DeeDee's daughter, LeeAnn, was a real piece of work. She hadn't had to deal with any rules for most of her life, and it showed. She not only inherited her mom's short and stocky stature but also her addictive personality. LeeAnn had dropped out of high school and didn't work, so she spent most days in the house smoking pot and most nights drinking. She had a deadbeat boyfriend who went out to the bars until all hours, and if he didn't find someone else to go home with, he'd settle for her after last call. DeeDee knew all this and didn't give a lick.

For all her faults, DeeDee was at least working. In fact, she was the only one in the house who was gainfully employed, at two part-time jobs: one making submarine sandwiches at a sub shop and another working in customer service at Sears.

Craig spent the days drinking and the nights drinking even more. Bottles just accumulated wherever he went, and they stayed there until someone else cleaned them up. He was a lazy slob in nearly everything he did, including not even bothering to wash his clothes. He just wore the same dirty ones day after day.

One thing he was a master at, however, was scheming. He came up with all kinds of crazy plans, and some of them he even pulled off. That was usually how he made money to fund his drinking. I didn't have a job on the Cape, and I really needed some cash, so when Craig told me about his big idea, I was all ears.

Craig was a genius with cars. He could take a car that hadn't worked for years and bring it back from the dead in a matter of minutes. He'd noticed that in the area where we were living towing companies charged a fee of up to $100 to take unwanted cars away. So we put an ad in the paper that said, "We take junk cars away for free."

The calls came in before the ink could even dry. And when they did, we would drive over to the caller's house in an unregistered car with some unknown or expired license plates so nobody could trace us. If people were looking to get rid of a car that didn't run, Craig would do some work on it so that we could drive it off the property. He did that again and again and again.

Once we got it on our property, we fixed it up and sold it. I would go into the junkyard and cut out an old inspection sticker from an abandoned car and tape it on the window of the car we were selling. Or other times we would just take cars from the junkyard and fix them up to sell. We were like the MacGyvers of the car-scheming world, using all kinds of household items to get them up and running. Coat hangers did a whiz-bang job of holding the frame together, or keeping the muffler on. Cardboard pizza boxes came in handy for body work: we would take part of the box and cover whatever spot or hole needed covering, tape over it with duct tape, and then spray paint it enough so you couldn't tell.

Once the car was working, we would put another ad in the paper to find a buyer. Our sales ranged from a couple hundred dollars to a couple thousand, and our supply was limitless. As far as I was concerned, it was a pretty brilliant plan.

When we weren't selling other people's cars, we were defrauding supermarkets. Back then the stores issued check cards that allowed you to get up to $50 cash and an unlimited amount of groceries if you wrote a check. Craig discovered that they didn't do any kind of credit check, so anyone with a checking account could get a card. He went around to different stores, got the $50 in cash, and waited around to see how long it would take for them to discover that he didn't have any money in his account to cover it. He found that, on average, it took three weeks. And by the time one supermarket notified him that he owed them money, his wallet was full of cash that he got from writing new checks at other supermarkets. Using the old robbing-Peter-to-pay-Paul scheme, he used one supermarket's cash to pay off another supermarket.

The system made sense to me, so I joined him. After a while, we said the hell with it and stopped covering the debts we owed. We hit all the supermarkets we could in Massachusetts and Rhode Island, writing false checks and walking out with cash and groceries. Between that and the car circuit, it was enough to get by for a good six, seven months.

As they say, however, all good things must come to an end, and it wasn't long before the stores finally caught on and canceled our cards. That's when I learned that Craig had actually served time in jail for check fraud already. Combine that with the fact that I was still on probation from my last arrest, and things didn't look good. If I was found guilty of any more offenses, my suspended sentence could be activated. I told Craig I was going to try to lay low for a while.

That phrase had always been the death knell for me. Whenever I said I was going to lay low, something bad was bound to happen. This time, it was another accident. I cut someone off, and in doing so, a car hit the front of my vehicle. I got knocked into the next lane, causing a five-car pileup.

My car was one of those Craig-and-Jay specials, straight out of the junkyard, covered in pizza boxes and spray paint, but it held together good enough. I pulled over to the side of the road with the rest of the people who were involved, and we exchanged information. I showed them my registration, and fortunately there was nothing visible on it to indicate that it had been canceled. One of the guys that had been involved in the accident wanted to do things the right way, so he insisted that we wait for the cops to show up. I cringed at the idea and headed back to my car.

That's when I started to get nervous. I was hung over, stoned, my registration was no good, I had no insurance, and my driver's license had been revoked thanks to a pile of unpaid parking tickets. I was like a sitting duck, getting more and more freaked out as the minutes ticked by.

So I took off. I sped away and then pulled off the freeway. I hid my car in a parking lot, so the cops couldn't find it, and called Craig to come pick me up. A few days went by and I hadn't heard anything from the cops. I felt safe enough to retrieve my car and parked it in the dirt driveway alongside the house. That's when the cops showed up. I heard the car pull up outside and watched as the police officer surveyed the vehicle. Then he walked up to the door, and I told LeeAnn to answer it. While she talked to the cop, I sat on the other side of the wall drinking Bloody Marys with about four or five shots of vodka.

"Where's Jay?" he asked. "What happened to the car?"

She did a good job of lying. She told them she didn't know anything about the car and insisted that I wasn't there. She was actually pretty convincing about it. I had my doubts about the kid's skill sets, but if she ever wanted to pursue a life of lies and crime, she'd probably do a bang-up job.

The cop didn't bother coming back, but a couple days later I got citations in the mail for hit-and-run and leaving the scene of an accident. I appeared in front of the court for the hearing and explained that I left because I was sick and I had to go to the bathroom real bad. They accepted my reason without question, and I got off. Again. They didn't even ask to see my registration or proof of insurance.

♦

As part of my resolution to stay out of trouble, I got a legitimate job as a bouncer at Fiddlebees, one of the local nightclubs. It didn't pay much, but it put me in the midst of a giant party where I got to drink free of charge. It was pretty perfect, as jobs go. The hours were late night—Thursday through Sunday from 9:00 p.m. to 1:30 a.m.—and their only request of the staff was that we wait an hour after we started our shift to start drinking. I didn't always honor the rule, but I did appreciate it.

When the shift ended, I usually stayed on with a few others and kept throwing 'em back. By law, we weren't supposed to be there past two, but if the cops drove by, we'd all just dive behind the bar and hide. It wasn't uncommon for the cleaning crew to find us still there drinking at six in the morning.

Cocaine went hand in hand with the nightclub scene, and that made the job an even better fit for me. I hadn't done much coke since I'd arrived on the Cape. Not because I was on a health kick, I just couldn't find a dealer. Now I was back, and what a beautiful reunion it was. It felt just like it did when I got high back in the early years—that euphoric kind of high I'd always been chasing.

I started cozying up to a tall, thin guy named Timmy. He was always drinking; that was how he got his business done, selling cocaine at the bar. Before long I was wheeling and dealing right along with him. I'd buy a little bit at a time, keeping some and selling the rest. I never had to worry about keeping too much for myself. As the doorman, patrons knew that if they tipped me with some of their stash or bought me a shot they could get in without a cover charge. It was a powerful position to be in, and as a guy who was still pretty socially awkward and obese, I loved the attention.

I ended up renting an apartment at the back of the club. It was great for my social life. I was meeting all kinds of people at the bar—bartenders, musicians, DJs, and women. Having an apartment so close by meant I could invite dates over and throw parties, and it was all within crawling distance.

The owner of the bar, Mark, lived near me, and I saw a lot of him. He drank with us every night, and even drunk we could see he had a drinking problem. One night when he was good and hammered, he told us he knew that a lot of people who were working for him there were ripping him off. He didn't like it, he said, but as long as they stayed his drinking buddies, he would put up with it. It was a pretty sad thing to hear. It was like the money was some kind of hush-currency he was willing to pay to have drinking friends.

After hours, we were always coming up with some crazy ideas. One night, Timmy and I got to talking about grilling and sauces. He told me about a recipe he had for shish kebabs and some great sauces he'd made. The discussion somehow took me back to my childhood. I hadn't thought about it in years, but all of a sudden I remembered how much I'd loved cooking as a kid. Food had always been so much more than food to me, probably because of my mom. It was emotions, escape, love, creativity, art. It was a way of sharing something from the heart and making other people happy, and it was something that I had a natural talent for.

I'd shoved all those skills and all those memories away once I got into drugs and drinking. Long ago I'd stopped experimenting in the kitchen. The only thing I heated anymore was cocaine. Talking about it brought it all back. I had a sudden itch to create something, to cook, to share again.

The more Timmy and I discussed it the more enthusiastic I became.

"What if we set up a gas grill on the deck outside?" I suggested. "I could grill up all kinds of stuff, bring a new clientele into the place."

We talked about it long into the night. Timmy loved the idea. I would call it the Grill Deck, I told him. I thought maybe I was really on to something.

This was the first time since I was a kid that I had been enthusiastic about something positive, something not related to drugs or alcohol. So I took it and ran with it. I proposed the idea to Mark, and he actually agreed to let me do it. I could hardly believe it. After being a complete screwup for so long, I was now looking at the opportunity I'd always wanted but never knew I needed. I'd dreamed of owning my own business but never had the confidence or drive to do anything about it. Now, combining business with cooking, something clicked inside me. My life suddenly had a passion and a purpose—and a whole list of things to do in order to get this thing up and running.

I bought the grill and put up flyers for the grand opening. I threw myself into it completely: booked a guitarist, bought the food, and started prepping. My specialty was different kinds of shish kebabs. I marinated the different meats—lamb, beef, chicken—in teriyaki, spicy barbeque, and blush wine sauces. The vegetables soaked in Italian dressing. I bought corn on the cob and rice to be served on the side. And then I waited for the Sunday opening.

Sunday morning came and it rained like crazy, like I hadn't seen it rain in months. *This is a catastrophe*, I thought, and popped open a beer to console myself. *No one will come out in the rain.*

For about a second I thought about canceling, but quickly reconsidered. I figured I'd be hanging out at the bar that night anyway. I figured I might as well be productive and go through with the original plan.

I'm glad I did, because I couldn't have been more wrong. It was a packed house. I ended up moving the grill indoors and customers piled in and ordered kebabs right and left. I manned the grill while chatting with the customers, watching their faces as they tried my food. They lit up with each bite, reminding me why I loved cooking.

Mark was thrilled at the turnout, just as he should have been. This day was shaping into the best Sunday the club had ever had. And it was all because I was there, doing what I loved. He encouraged me to keep up the good work.

The honeymoon stage lasted a couple of weeks. Then a couple of business issues cropped up in the form of the fire marshal. The issues were all technicalities: an ordinance that prohibited gas grills on decks, and a mandate that said I couldn't use a household appliance for a commercial endeavor. Until I made some changes, he said, he was shutting me down.

In the past, something like that would have been a defeat. I would have gotten drunk and high and just moved on to the next thing. But something happened when I started cooking. I found a new drive and a new energy. Maybe it was because I had my own business and had no one to depend on but myself. Whatever it was, this was the first time that I resolved to constructively solve a problem.

The Grill Deck stayed open through the end of summer. But by then Mark had been having a lot of business troubles, and they went way beyond a couple of employees stealing from him. He declared bankruptcy and told me the restaurant portion had to go; he didn't want competition to the food he was offering inside. I was heartbroken. It was my baby, after all, but there wasn't anything I could do.

He kept Fiddlebees open and let me go back to my job as a bouncer, but it was just too much for me. I was so depressed about the restaurant closing that I could barely bring myself to leave my apartment. I was lost in a fog of drugs, pollution, haze, alcohol, fear, and stagnation and just wasn't fit to be in the public anymore. Mark had always been a reasonable guy, and he always gave me a lot of leeway, but once I stopped showing up for work, I was out. The message was clear, from one addict to another: you're fired.

I could no longer afford the apartment, so I moved into a rooming house that charged $65 a week, and I filed for unemployment. It didn't take long to realize that a man cannot get by on $100 a month, so I started selling coke again. Timmy fronted me the stuff and I paid him back after I made a few sales. It was pretty small-time, nothing like what I used to do. My only real goal was to sell enough to feed my own habits. But even that became a lot to ask after a while.

If I were to take a snapshot of my life at that point in time, it would have included the bottle, the pipe, and a whole lot of self-pity. I was back to the same ground zero I'd been at a hundred times before: I had no family or friends, no job, no money, no possessions. All of my time was spent indulging my addictions. It was like I'd turned into one of those Whac-A-Mole machines you see at video arcades. My addictions were the pesky little critter, and every time they'd come up I'd have to beat them back down. No sooner did I solve one problem than the next one popped up. Oops, there's coke! Oops, there's liquor! Bam, bam! Knock 'em down!

My life had become a big cycle of craving and failed attempts at fulfilling those cravings. I'd stay up all night freebasing and then wait for the neighborhood liquor store to open at eight in the morning to get my bottle of whiskey. I mixed it with ginger ale, just like my old man used to drink, and then I drank until I fell asleep or passed out. When I woke up, I did it all over again. Sometimes, however, I'd go twenty-four, thirty-six, even forty-eight hours without sleeping.

I was living in such a fog that once again I stopped showering, stopped doing laundry, stopped taking out the trash. And this, inevitably, brought me back to rock bottom. To the moment where it was up to me to decide whether I lived or died. Brought me back to the precipice, to Machu Picchu.

I was just about out of cash and totally out of hope. The only dependable things in my life were my substances, and even they weren't exactly holding up their end of the bargain lately. That's when I walked into the 19th Hole, ordered a beer, and was unexpectedly faced with that life-changing decision to drink or not to drink.

I wanted to feel better, wanted to drink it, to tell you the God's honest truth. I was hardwired to drink. I mean this is what I *did*. This was *it*. But I took one look at it, one smell of it, one taste of it, and I just couldn't. This wasn't living.

You might expect me to recount that there was some kind of angst or sweat or firecrackers or struggle indicating the gravity of the decision I was making. But the fact of the matter was I just didn't want that beer. This was my moment of clarity. So I walked out. It was May 28, 1991. I was twenty-nine years old.

I got back to my tiny room and sat and thought. This was where it started getting scary. I hadn't really considered the next step beyond throwing that bottle away. I wasn't exactly sure where to begin. *What should I do next? What did people do next?* I knew I had to do something because if I didn't, it was only a matter of time before that beer would taste good again.

I remembered back to when I was standing in the unemployment line. I'd filled out some forms for a pilot program that gave health insurance to the unemployed. For some reason, I had a feeling the answer was in that packet. So I searched and found the papers, and then I called to see if the insurance covered treatment for addictions.

My hunch was right. When I got through, I found out that it did, indeed, cover treatment. The woman on the phone explained that my coverage included up to fourteen days of inpatient care at a nearby facility. She checked around for availability, only to find that at the moment they had no openings.

"You'll have to wait until a bed becomes available," she told me.

I knew I could wait. My old, reliable, lifelong luck was still with me. Even in sobriety.

CHAPTER 8

I HUNG TIGHT FOR a few days before getting a call from a facility called McClain's. It was located nearby, in a suburb of Boston, and ran a fourteen-day in-house treatment program. They were ready for me right away—and I could say the same for me. Since putting down that drink I had had no second thoughts, but I was in desperate need of some guidance and community. The next day I took a bus to the treatment center.

McClain's was huge and sat on an expansive campus. As I walked up, I liked that it looked like a series of old-fashioned houses. It felt comfortable, almost homey. The inside was somewhere in between a recovery house and a hospital, depending on the area and the seriousness of the patients' problems. The psychiatric patients, for example, were in a ward that felt pretty sterile. Fortunately, I wasn't assigned to that area. They put me in a more laid-back wing of the facility.

They told me the rules at check-in: no using, and no physical contact with other patients. Seemed fair to me. One of the staff led me to my room and introduced me to my roommate, an overweight guy with black hair who made a living by selling hotdogs and sausages off a cart outside a hospital. He was friendly enough, and from past experience I knew it could have been much, much worse.

After a quick tour, I pretty much crawled into bed and stayed there. Seemed like that was all I did for the first three days: sleep and eat. I'd wake up and head to the cafeteria for three meals a day, and I'd get up to use the bathroom, but other than that I was in bed. I was exhausted, and it was the kind of exhaustion that wouldn't go away even if I were to sleep twenty-four hours straight.

Sleeping led to horrible, vivid nightmares as the toxins worked their way out of my system, but even that didn't dampen my resolve. It was the best way available to escape the horrors of withdrawal symptoms. Mine were pretty intense. For nearly five days my digestive tract was wracked with cramps and relentless diarrhea, and I was sweating uncontrollably. It was all normal detox stuff, something every recovering addict suffers in one way or another, but man was it rough.

I guess the worst thing was, once I got there, I didn't want to be there. Not because I wanted to run to the nearest bar or anything. The second I had put that beer down I really was committed to quitting. But it was all so new and different and regimented. I'd lived without rules for so long that once they were placed on me I didn't want to walk their walk and I didn't want to talk their talk. I had a bad attitude and I didn't give a damn.

I think part of it was because I still had so many drugs remaining in my system. Regular drug screenings were part of the requirements of the program, and when they gave me a test a few days after my arrival, my results actually came in so high that they accused me of using. I was that toxic.

After those three days of catching up on sleep, they told me it was time I started attending group therapy sessions. I wasn't enthused about it, but I knew it was the right thing to do. I was feeling real low, depressed. Every time I looked in the mirror I expected to see some kind of giant hole, devoid of energy and life. They all told me it was normal, and it was going to get better. The counselors said it, the other patients said it, the recovery community said it. But they all stressed that it was going to take time. It's like if you bang your head with a hammer over and over again, it's still going to hurt after you stop.

At the heart of it all, I knew these feelings of being lost and sad weren't new; I just wasn't accustomed to actually confronting them. Since I was twelve I'd always relied on something else to camouflage my feelings. Now, if I was really going to change my life, I had no choice but to deal with them.

A counselor named Wilson led my therapy sessions. He was this very short, analytical Poindexter kind of guy. I liked him and I liked the way he talked about things. They made sense. Basically, he introduced the principles of the twelve-step program. It was stuff that I'd heard for almost all my life, but for the first time I actually listened.

He told me that the first thing I had to do was admit that I'd lost the ability to control my addictions and that my life had become unmanageable. To me, that was pretty much a given. I'd lost my job, my apartment, my friends, and my family. I'd gone down so low I had nothing else to lose. Unmanageable seemed like an understatement.

Step two took a little more thought. It called upon me to recognize a power outside of myself that could give me strength. I was a little worried by that one. Even though I'm Jewish, I had never been into the religious aspect of my culture. I'd been forced to go through the motions of Judaism as a kid, but it never really stuck. I told Wilson that, and he explained that it wasn't mandatory to get my strength from God per se; it just had to come from something other than myself. He said people in the past had picked all kinds of things for their source of strength, ranging from the therapy group to something as simple as a lightbulb. The important thing, he said, was to find something that worked for me.

I liked that. Religious or not, I did believe that there had to be something out there that was greater than ourselves. How else could you explain our presence here? The Earth's presence? The Moon's presence? Something was responsible for it.

The therapy—and there was a lot of therapy during my stay—helped open my mind and eased a lot of my anxiety. After having been drunk or high for so many years, I honestly didn't know how to live sober. I sure as hell couldn't fathom being sober for the rest of my life—it was just too much, too soon. Thanks to the guidance I got during my sessions, I started to think about the importance of taking it one day at a time, one hour at a time, one minute at a time. "Yesterday is history and tomorrow is a mystery, so all you have is today." That was one of the mantras.

I also had to start taking responsibility for who I was and where I was going. I couldn't blame anybody but myself for the things I'd done that landed me here. It wasn't about the people I'd met, the places I'd been, or the things I'd seen. It was about me and my choices. It was about my inability to control myself.

Cliché or not, this was the beginning of the rest of my life. It was my chance to make a fresh start, to learn about who I was and why I'd gotten here, and to understand why this—sobriety—was better than the alternative. As I spent more time in the program, I started to feel something that I had barely recognized at first. It was a sense that I hadn't had in years. I felt *safe*. I was living in a place where the schedule was the same every day, the meals were provided, the bed was warm, and the priority was to help me help myself. It was stable, comfortable, reliable. I started getting to know some of the other patients, and we all had similar experiences, similar war stories. It was my third time in rehab, and I finally felt like I was really making progress. That's because I had made the call this time. I was the one who was ready.

Before I knew it, ten days had passed, and Wilson informed me that my insurance company had requested me to check out. Although this was a fourteen-day program, my insurance company seemed to think I was cured after ten.

I told him I didn't want to go. He said that he and the other counselors agreed that I wasn't ready to be back on my own. But unless I had the funds to pay for it myself, there was nothing they could do. Before I left, he promised that they would help me explore other more affordable options, like a halfway house.

"Nah," I said, shrugging him off. "I'm ready to go back to Cape Cod and work my bar job. I'll stay sober. I'll be fine."

The idea of going back to a halfway house really sickened me. Sure, I was starting to feel comfortable in rehab, but I wasn't ready for something like that again. I didn't want to be lumped in with a bunch of losers. I just wanted to get back into the real world.

Wilson wasn't having it.

"The program works if you work the program," he told me. "What you really need is the kind of support network that a halfway house offers. Returning to your old life in a bar, surrounded by your old using partners, is the worst thing you could do to yourself right now."

Even with ten-plus days under my belt, I was still waging a war when it came to sobriety. I knew that 90 percent of alcoholics didn't stay sober the first time they tried, and most rehab programs saw a relapse rate that was around 50 percent. The more I thought about it, Wilson was right to be concerned. Right now, the only thing I had in the world was my sobriety. If keeping it meant going to a halfway house, then that was what I would do. I agreed to it.

The transition counselor looked around the area for an available bed, and found nothing. So she had my name put on a waiting list and told me it could be a good six weeks before anything turned up. I just had to find a place to stay in the meantime.

Now that I was properly frightened about what would happen if I went back to Cape Cod, I scratched that off my list. I was still on shaky grounds with my parents, so I didn't want to contact them unless it was an absolute emergency.

Not sure of what else to do, I got on a bus and headed to the South End of Boston, where I knew there was a Salvation Army homeless shelter. They had a bed available, so I stayed the night in a giant, gym-sized room full of cots. I was surrounded by destitute souls who carried all of their belongings around in a single bag. Many of them were mentally ill and didn't even seem to notice when a large rat scurried across the floor right past them.

If I were to continue on my same reckless path, I knew that this was the kind of place I would probably land, and the thought terrified me. I tucked the memory away, ready to pull it out if I ever thought about straying from the straight and narrow.

And then I called my parents. I didn't want to stay here any longer. I wanted to go home.

♦

My parents agreed to let me stay with them until a bed opened up at a halfway house, under one condition: I had to attend recovery meetings during my stay. I happily agreed. It was the first time in my life that I was actually determined to abide by all of their rules.

It wasn't easy being home, being in that familiar environment. I was still craving drugs, still craving a drink, but I resisted temptation. Instead, when those feelings arose, I would head to a meeting and glean some kind of inner strength. The important thing was that despite my cravings, I wanted to stay sober more than I wanted to use.

Then a bed opened up at Hospitality House, a transitional house in Hopkinton, about forty minutes from my parents' house. I had to admit I was actually disappointed when the call came. I had been doing well with my parents, and my feelings toward the idea of a halfway house still hadn't changed.

When I got there, the manager, Daniel, greeted me at the door. He was this heavy guy with stringy brown hair, wearing an untucked shirt and dirty jeans. He was exactly the kind of lowlife I would have expected to find there in an old, rundown house. He gave me a tour of the three-story building, with its dated kitchen and mismatched furniture, and then he took me to my room, which I would be sharing with three other guys. That, apparently, was how all the new residents started out.

As I was putting my clothes away, Daniel ran through the rules. I was expected to attend at least one recovery meeting a day, outside of the house, in addition to a weekly recovery meeting in the house. I was also expected to work. If I didn't have a job, I was required to spend my days looking for one. It was against the rules to hang out at the house during the day, and any drug or alcohol use was a one-way ticket out of there.

It was better than the Salvation Army, but not by much. My room-mates had been better back when I was a drunk. Here, my housemates were a mix of guys fresh out of prison, homeless drunks just off the streets, and every kind of white trash you could imagine. *They belong here,* I thought to myself, *I don't.* As if I didn't feel like enough of a loser and a failure before coming here, now I had to be surrounded by this baloney.

I was so busy hating my situation that I didn't make any kind of effort to get a job. Instead, I hid out in the library during the day. At night, I dutifully attended meetings and listened to people telling stories of triumph over their addictions. The stories were vivid, powerful, and emotional—and I didn't believe them. Not one word. I heard story after story about people who'd spent years away from drugs and alcohol and claimed that they were happy. I was convinced that they were lying to themselves and to us.

But then, without warning, the chip started melting off my shoulder and something started seeping in. Maybe it was me who'd been lying to myself. Maybe these people really were happy. In spite of myself, their stories began to touch me. I kept hearing the same phrases, over and over, like "just keep coming until you come to believe," and the more meetings I attended the more I did believe. Before long I was an all-out convert. I suddenly wanted their lives. I wanted the life of the doctor who stayed sober and the construction worker who stayed clean. I wanted their freedom, their joy, their triumph, their clearheadedness. I wanted their sobriety.

I had a radical change of heart, and it was exactly what I needed. Being sober wasn't just about not drinking and not using. It wasn't just about the things I *didn't* have; it was about the things that were now within reach—love, happiness, wealth. These people I listened to night after night had everything they wanted, but they couldn't have these things until they were sober. It was a trade-off—their dark, depressing, toxic lives in exchange for hope and dreams, hard work, and, hopefully, fulfillment.

And just like that, I was inspired to get my life together. I finally went out and looked for a job, but as hard as I tried, I couldn't find one I could keep. I didn't want to violate the rules of the house, and figuring that I'd gotten what I needed—a positive attitude and renewed determination, I decided it was time to move on. After three months in that halfway house, I moved back to Boston, where I knew I could get a job, and lived with my parents again.

I found work as the manager/bagel maker at Rosenburg Bagels. I was happy to be working with food again, and most of the time the job was great. That is, until I got a little too close to the heavy machinery.

I was working with the veteran bagel maker, Kyle. It was a steamer of a day, and as we tried to get the bagel dough to go through the machine, it kept sticking, so we were pushing it through manually. Right in the middle of making egg bagels, with my hand stuck all the way inside this machine, it started moving. I heard a pop, felt a burst of pressure, and then just saw blood—blood pooling at the bottom of the machine and then mixing in with the dough. It was like watching a horror movie.

We stopped the machine and I pulled my hand out. Part of my index finger was gone. It had been smashed, cut off just above the second knuckle.

Kyle had the presence of mind to save my mangled, amputated fingertip and called the paramedics. An ambulance rushed me to the hospital, and the next thing I knew, I woke up from surgery to a bandaged left hand—they weren't able to reattach the fingertip—and a morphine drip going into my arm.

I stared at the morphine machine. As the drugs pumped into me I nearly laughed at the irony of the situation. Try as I might to stay away from mind-altering substances, they were now being fed directly into my bloodstream. I'd told the doctor that I was in recovery, but he decided that the pain medications were a must to help me cope with the surgery and the pain. So I went along with it. A few years earlier I would have been stoked to have an accident that would get me a prescription for drugs. Now I was determined not to let them lead me astray from my hard-fought sobriety.

Jay Littmann in his hometown of Everett, Massachusetts, at the age of five.

Jay and Monica Littmann were married at The Flamingo Las Vegas on May 16, 1998.

Monica, Jacob and Jay Littmann celebrating Jacob's first birthday
party at Monica's family's home in Mexico on January 3, 2001.

In the summer of 2006, Jay Littmann took his parents on an
all expenses paid cruise to Alaska. This photo was taken in the
private jet which they used to reach the ship.

Jay Littmann in his hometown of Everett, Massachusetts, at the age of five.

Jay and Monica Littmann were married at The Flamingo Las Vegas on
May 16, 1998.

Monica, Jacob and Jay Littmann celebrating Jacob's first birthday party at Monica's family's home in Mexico on January 3, 2001.

In the summer of 2006, Jay Littmann took his parents on an all expenses paid cruise to Alaska. This photo was taken in the private jet which they used to reach the ship.

Courtesy Erik Kabik Photography

Jay Littmann posing outside of his booth during the 2009 Mr. Olympia Weekend held in Las Vegas, Nevada. Featured in this photo are two of Jay's exotic cars including his 2010 Lamborghini Gallardo LP560-4 Spyder and his 2010 Ferrari Scuderia Spider 16m.

Courtesy Erik Kabik Photography

Chef Jay Littmann donates 9,000 of his protein-fortified "Lite Bites" cookies to the Chefs for Kids program. These cookies were distributed to low-income schools throughout Clark County.

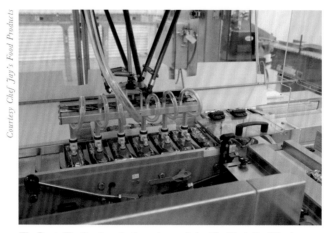

The Presto Top Loader robotic equipment helps Chef Jay's Food Products maximize productivity while eliminating human contact with his product.

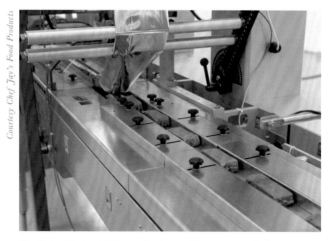

The Doboy Horizontal Flow packaging machine wraps protein bars at speeds of up to 400 bars per minute.

CHAPTER 9

I WASN'T IN ANY shape to work after I left the hospital, so I used the time to really concentrate on making myself better. I began taking a more active role at meetings, and I signed up for different duties, such as leading the meeting or just making coffee for it. It was a small step, but it made me feel involved and accountable.

Between meetings, I continued cleaning up the messy trail of wreckage I'd created. I'd been mentally checked out for so long, there was a whole lot of financial and legal stuff to take care of. First, I needed to get my driver's license back. I had more than $2,000 in overdue fines all over the state, and each jurisdiction required that I pay their fines in person. So I traveled up and down Massachusetts making payments. It took a lot of time and painstaking legwork, but once I was done, I got my license so I could legally drive again.

Next point of business was back taxes. I had actually never filed my own income taxes: my dad had filed them for me until I turned eighteen, and after that I was on my own. Only I never bothered to do it. If you think one year of taxes is a pain, try eleven! I was worried that I would owe the government thousands and thousands of dollars, but amazingly, I ended up actually getting a refund.

Then I started tackling my abysmal credit rating. I'd messed up my credit score back when I was a teenager. I had never bothered paying back the car loan my dad had cosigned, and it didn't help my score when I defaulted on my student loans. At one point, my credit score was so low that I couldn't even rent a television from one of those rent-to-own places. I'd long given up on using my Social Security number, and for a while I actually switched over to using my little brother's instead. I gave it to the phone company once, so I could get service, and then I never bothered to pay the bills. A collections agency went after him. In hindsight, I was a real peach.

I had a lot of reparations to make and I did the best I could. I was getting a small amount of money, thanks to the workers' comp payments I received each week because of my mishap at the bagel shop. I put most of that money toward my loans, fines, fees, etc. My earnings actually stretched further than I expected. Living life was much cheaper without the expense of drugs and alcohol.

Nine months somehow flew by, and by that time I had really started to feel better, more like a functioning human being. Three months later, May 31, 1992, I hit the one-year mark. It was a big deal, being sober 365 days. As a kind of reward to myself, I quit smoking and started working out. I went at it with the same ferocity I went at everything, and before long I was running three to five miles a day and lifting weights. It took me until age thirty to learn that it was actually possible to feel good from doing healthy things.

Right after my first year of sobriety, I started thinking about what I wanted to do next. I knew that the thing that made me the happiest over the years had been food. What I really wanted to do was go to culinary school to become a chef. I just didn't have the money to do it.

Then I heard about a state program called Mass Rehab, which assisted recovering addicts and alcoholics in going back to school. I applied for it, but I didn't get accepted. That made me want it even more. I waited and applied again. It took months and months, but they finally took me on.

Because the state program would help me financially only with tuition at an in-state school, I enrolled at Newbury College in Boston. It was January 1993, and I could barely believe that just two years prior I had been living like a vagrant, unable to do anything remotely good for myself. Now I felt like I had a beautiful blank slate before me, just waiting to be filled.

◆

As a student I lived with a few roommates in a sober house—although it often seemed like I was the only sober one. I didn't see anyone drinking there, but I heard rumors. I grew more and more suspicious when my things started disappearing. First, it was a gold chain. Then, my wallet disappeared. I didn't want any part of that kind of scene so I moved out.

I didn't want to move in with my parents. I'd burdened them for many years, and to return there would be hard on all of us. I'd been spending a lot of time in and out of meetings getting to know a guy name Stan. He was a big, burly guy like me, a tough union rep from south Boston. Stan was in his upper fifties and had been sober fourteen years at that point. I got the sense that he may have been involved in some way with organized crime, but he'd traded it all in to get clean. Once we established a comfort level I asked him if he'd be my sponsor, and he agreed. He was pretty involved in my life, so when I told him about what was going on at the "sober" house, he offered me a place to stay for a while.

I moved in immediately and knew it was the right decision from the get-go. We had some good talks. He really taught me about the value of living honestly with others and, most of all, being honest with yourself. He told me some of the things that had helped him stay sober as long as he had: staying out of bars, not hanging out with anyone who uses, and helping other addicts to do the same. The stuff Stan said really stuck. The supportive environment was just what I needed.

Culinary school kept me pretty busy. I was in class about eight hours a day during the week, and then I drove a cab about forty to forty-five hours Thursday through Sunday. I managed to study between fares, and that semester my grades were good enough to get me on the dean's list.

Over the summer I dug out my old real estate license and took a job with my childhood pal Johnny's agency. I focused on renting out apartments around Boston. With all the college students moving in for the summer, it was easy to bring in between $1,000 and $2,000 a week all summer long. It felt great to finally have some cash in my bank account.

After my tuition was paid I even had enough left over to finance my first new car. Yes, I said finance. I could barely believe it when I learned my credit was good enough to actually get a loan. I put the money toward a black 1994 Mitsubishi Galant. I was floored at how good it felt to actually drive a car legally. This was far more than just a car to me. It was a symbol of my sobriety, and a reminder of how different my life was now that I'd become a responsible and active part of it.

My next step, in order to graduate culinary school, was to complete an externship, meaning I had to find a job in the culinary field. I applied for a position as a head chef/manager at a camp for children in rural Maine. Sure, I had very limited experience with managing, and even less experience working with kids, but that's not what I told them. My fast-talking skills took over during the interview, and I filled them in on my management experience at the bagel shop, leaving out the injury and the fact that I was there a very short time. I told them about my days at the Grill Deck to illustrate my extensive cooking skills, and I padded my resume and just generally talked a good rap.

Somehow, it worked. They agreed to take me on, and I figured I'd just wing it. It hadn't failed me yet. I drove out to the middle of nowhere to get to the camp, and I was relieved to find that all of the cooks working under me knew far more than I did, so I could rely on them to teach me.

My boss made it clear that my main priority was to keep expenditures under budget. He gave me a menu from previous years to use as a guide, and I started cutting costs right away. It was the little things that made a big difference, like changing some meals from chicken breasts to chicken pieces and introducing new, inexpensive options like BLT sandwiches and other kid-friendly meals.

The job lasted three months, and while I was there, I lived in a small house in the woods. I hadn't spent much time in nature before, but I really enjoyed the peacefulness of the wilderness. It also felt good to throw myself into work and be completely separated from the temptations of my old life. Once a week I would leave camp to attend a recovery meeting, just to keep me on my toes.

By the time camp ended, I'd saved them more than $10,000. My boss's boss gave me a $500 bonus, and I got an A on the externship paper I had to write. I felt appreciated and accomplished, and I knew the path I'd taken was the right one.

◆

Fresh out of culinary school—from which I graduated magna cum laude—and having been sober for more than four years, I figured there would be no better time than that moment to make a change. (Of course, having to dig my car out of heavy Boston snows at least nine times that winter might have influenced my decision a little too!)

I craved a warmer climate like Los Angeles. I was getting pretty heavily into weightlifting, and I thought it would be fun to live near Venice Beach, also known as Muscle Beach, and located near the original Gold's Gym. So, on January 2, 1995, I loaded up the Mitsubishi and headed west. I stopped in Las Vegas, expecting to stay a few days with this guy John, who was a friend of my aunt's. John took me on a tour around town, and as we got to know one another I learned that he knew some people in the culinary field. He offered to help make some connections if I wanted to find a job there. I thought about it as I drove up and down the Strip, envisioning a glamorous life working at Caesars Palace or one of the other mega-resorts. It was a tempting offer. California was in a recession and Vegas was booming, so it made more sense to stay there and get some experience before continuing on to California when the economy got better.

My first priority was to find a cheap place to live. I answered a few ads and met some strange landlords (picture a woman in a bathrobe drinking a screwdriver while six dogs yapped at her feet) and saw some abysmal accommodations (a dingy room with an army cot) but finally found a place that at least seemed passable for only $350 a month. It wasn't until I moved in, however, that I discovered there was only one bathroom for five people, including the owner who lived in a closet and some guy who lived in a toolshed in the backyard. Until I could find a job and afford a better place, it would have to do.

The more John told me about the executive chef at Caesars Palace, the more I wanted to work with him. The guy had a pretty inspirational story. He'd started at the bottom, as a food runner, but he worked hard and climbed his way up to the department's top position. Hearing that, I figured he was the type of man who would give a guy a chance. John lined up an interview so I could go meet him.

I arrived early, hoping to make a good impression.

"You're early. I'm not ready yet," he greeted me.

It wasn't the great start I was hoping for. The negativity continued throughout the interview. He asked me what experience I had, and I started to outline where I'd worked in Boston, when he interrupted me.

"No. What experience do you have locally?"

I explained that I had just graduated culinary school at the top of my class and moved here. I hadn't found a job yet.

"Culinary school doesn't matter," he said. "Job experience is what counts. Come back after you get some experience."

I tried not to let that response get to me. I spent the next few days interviewing whenever and wherever I could. I wasn't the only person who thought his dream job was behind the golden doors of a casino, though; it was a highly competitive process. There were days when I waited hours and hours for an interview, only to be turned away and told that with all the people applying, they'd run out of time to talk to me. There were a handful of jobs available and thousands of people who wanted them. Rejection became a daily routine.

Finally, after weeks of searching, I got a job at a catering company. I actually met my boss, Chef Russell, through a friend of mine in the recovery world. After years of attending meetings regularly, I was learning just how tight-knit the community was. If there's something you need, there's almost always someone in the group who has an answer. Even though I was new in town, I met people pretty quickly who were looking to help out one of their own. It was a good feeling.

Chef Russell was a great chef. He could make just about anything from memory and knew every cooking technique there was to know. Just watching him was like getting an education. His catering company handled high-end events. One of the first jobs I had with him was for the grand opening of Lake Las Vegas, a new luxury development, at the center of which was a manmade lake, about twenty miles southeast of the Strip. Standing there, you might as well have been in the Mediterranean, because it sure didn't feel like being in the middle of the desert with all those golf courses and lush lawns. Nevada Governor Kenny Guinn and Las Vegas Mayor Jan Jones arrived by helicopter, and much of the party took place on a large yacht.

We'd spent nearly a week in preparation, planning the menu, finding the best salmon to grill, and carving vegetables into the shape of birds for the table decorations. It went off without a hitch. After that, Chef Russell put me in charge of an employee dining room project for Bally Gaming. That one was a challenge because the slot machine manufacturing company didn't actually have a kitchen on-site. I found a nearby nightclub that would let me use their kitchen during the day, and then I'd pack it all into food warmers and drive it over to Bally in my car. It was a pretty involved process, and it tested my problem-solving skills, but I didn't mind problem solving, and I really liked having a steady gig.

Houses in Las Vegas were pretty affordable in the mid-1990s. It was actually possible to buy one for right around $100,000, which was far cheaper than the prices I was used to seeing in the Boston area. Now that my credit was on the upswing, buying a home was really starting to sound like the smart thing to do. I asked around and found out that culinary school attendance actually counted as work history on a mortgage application, so for the first time in my life I had a genuine list of jobs to draw on. Making money legally certainly had its perks.

I qualified for a HUD loan and found a four-bedroom house, with a pool, for $106,000 about fifteen minutes east of Las Vegas Boulevard. I put 3 percent down, and felt like I was on top of the world. Four years earlier I had been homeless. Now, I had my own home, my own swimming pool, and my own central air-conditioning!

Then I got laid off. The catering company was cutting expenses, and I was one of them. I shook it off, reminding myself it was a business decision, nothing personal. In the back of my mind I started planning to one day own my own business. If someone was going to control my destiny I wanted it to be me. It would take some time and money, of course, but I vowed one day I would do it.

In the meantime, I found a job as a cook during the graveyard shift at the Sourdough Café, a restaurant at Arizona Charlie's, which is known as a "locals" casino a few miles west of the Strip. The Sourdough Café, akin to a diner, was known for its inexpensive food—like the $1.99 breakfast specials—so I spent most of the night flipping eggs and bacon, making chicken fried steak and biscuits and gravy, and doing prep work for the next day. At $8 an hour, it was hardly the job I dreamed about when I was attending culinary school.

I was feeling pretty sorry for myself when my father called. He told me my mother might have cancer.

I booked a flight back to Boston immediately and took a leave of absence from my job. I stayed at my parents' house while we waited to learn more. The doctors were saying some pretty scary things, like they thought it was malignant.

When the test results come back we all breathed a sigh of relief. It wasn't cancer, after all, but a rare, treatable disorder that mimics cancer. They began treatment right away and said she'd be fine.

I was away so long that I lost my job at Arizona Charlie's, so I went back to driving a cab. I figured I didn't have anything to go back to, so I might as well stick around Boston awhile. I would at least be able to help out with my family and start saving money to put toward my own business.

By April I'd saved $10,000. I returned to Las Vegas with my savings and researched what kind of business I could open. I wanted it to be in the food industry, but I knew that it would have to be something unrelated to alcohol. I read everything I could get my hands on and found an ad in the local classifieds about a muffin shop that was for sale. *I could do that*, I thought to myself.

It was 1996, and I'd been noticing how popular bagels were becoming. I figured if I added those to the muffin menu I could really make a go of it. So I set up an appointment to meet with Merv, the owner, at the shop, which was called Mr. Muffin.

The run-down little storefront sat in a strip mall on the edge of Las Vegas' Chinatown, just a few blocks west of the Strip. My first thought when I walked in was, *Wow, this is . . . grungy.*

There were mountains of trash all over the place. Merv had refused to pay the fee they charged for commercial garbage service; he would just take it home and put it out with his personal trash. Thing is, he didn't bother taking it home more than a couple times a week. It was nasty, especially considering that the shop was only seven hundred square feet. I didn't want to think about how close that trash got to the food products, and I tried to put on my poker face to hide my disgust.

Five years prior, Merv had paid $35,000 and bought the business. Now he was just sick of it altogether, so he closed up the retail side of the shop and fired nearly everyone. He still had about a dozen wholesale accounts and was looking for the right person to take them over. He didn't want to make a profit off the sale; he was only looking to recoup what he'd spent and get rid of the headache. He was asking for $15,000 as a down payment, and then $20,000 more to be paid over three years.

I had my doubts. The piled-up trash really bothered me, as did the equipment, which consisted of two very old, decrepit ovens and one small, ancient twenty-quart mixer in disrepair. You had to keep a small bucket under it to catch the drips of oil that were leaking from it. There was also a grinder attachment that hooked on to the mixer. It was so old, Merv told me, that he could no longer get parts for it. Last time something broke he had to have a paddle specially made. For the life of me I couldn't figure out what he would need a grinder for in a muffin shop. When I asked him, he told me he used it to grind up all the old muffins and other leftover bakery items, which he then added to the batter of the new muffins. It was a pretty odd method. In fact, everything about the place was pretty odd. Did I really want to sink all of my savings into this?

On the other hand, it matched up perfectly with what I wanted in a business. It revolved around food, there wouldn't be a lot of inventory to keep, and raw bakery ingredients were fairly inexpensive. The rent was only $750 a month, and the overall price was within my budget. I figured that between credit cards and selling some stock holdings I could scrape up another $5,000 to add to my $10,000 in savings. At that moment, I really had no other options. So I did it. I got together the $15,000, handed it to Merv, and Mr. Muffin was mine. My lifelong dream had come true. I was my own boss.

Merv even agreed to stay on for a while just so he could show me the ropes. I was so green that I was relieved to have any kind of guidance. There was a lot to be done, but I wasn't afraid of hard work. I took it one step at a time, just like everything else. I cleaned the place from top to bottom, and started changing up the recipes a little, adding my own and getting rid of some of Merv's. I reopened the retail side of the business, selling coffee and pastries, because I figured every item I sold would help my bottom line. I brought in some tables and chairs and offered a nice spot for my customers to sit and chat.

Slowly, very slowly, people started coming into the shop. It wasn't happening nearly as fast as I wanted, partly because the place had no visible signage. I didn't know how Mr. Muffin had survived five years without it. I knew that unless people knew who I was and where I was, my muffin business would be toast.

So I talked to my landlord about it and he said he'd need to see a rendering before he could approve anything. I went to a sign company and explained what I wanted. They made a mock-up of a sign that pictured a large muffin man on a beige background with giant red letters that screamed out "Mr. Muffin." I took a computer printout of the sign to show my landlord. My plan was to fill the entire side of the one-story building with the sign, but I didn't tell the landlord that. He approved it, just as I'd hoped he would, no questions asked. Needless to say, a couple of days later he was not thrilled when he came in and saw the enormous sign. He yelled at me, but I told him it was his own fault. I'd done everything he'd asked. We left it at that, and business started picking up, at least a little bit, thanks to the new visual.

I hired a few different women who went around town selling individually wrapped baked goods from baskets they carried. They acted as independent contractors. I'd charge them $1 a cookie and they'd turn around and sell the cookie for $2. It took me awhile to find some good saleswomen, but before long I had a few aces that would bring in $50 to $100 a day. While they were out selling, I was baking, wrapping, labeling, and freezing things as fast as I could make them—which wasn't very fast at all considering my archaic equipment. I worked seven days a week, 60 hours altogether. It was the only way to run the place if I ever wanted to make a profit.

The items that seemed to be selling real well were a couple of holdover recipes from when Merv was there: healthy bars that came in oat and chocolate flavors. He had created them at the request of Healthy Connections, which was a diet and counseling business in Las Vegas. They were fat free and full of fiber, the kind of thing that was all the rage in the mid-1990s. When I came onboard they weren't even labeled, so the customers just referred to them as "fiber bars." We were also making fat-free muffins, cookies, and brownies for a few different health clubs, but nothing sold as well as those fiber bars.

Merv loathed those bars. Even though he'd created them, he acted as though they had been put on earth solely to torture him. At the time I took over, he was making about two dozen a week, but he wanted to phase out the bars because they were so high-maintenance to produce.

I understood where he was coming from. Making the bars was indeed a long, involved process. The dough was rich and about as thick as modeling clay, and because of my limited equipment I could make only enough of it to fill about a quarter of a sheet pan at a time. So I'd mound it on there and then take another sheet pan to mash it down and flatten it out. There were no eggs in it or anything, so it didn't have to be baked. Once it was in the pan I'd take a metal dough scraper, cut it all into rectangles and let them dry for a few hours. Then I would wrap them individually in Saran Wrap and freeze them, because if they were left at room temperature for more than a week they would spoil.

Despite all the work that went into them, I figured that we might really be on to something. I wanted to see if I could get them into more health food stores and gyms, so I designed a label for them that included their nutritional information, and I started calling them Oat Bars and Choc Bars.

I had just gotten an account to sell my products at the juice bars inside the local Gold's Gyms, so I approached one of the juice bar owners and gave him some free samples of the bars. He handed them out and was so impressed by the feedback he ordered three hundred bars to sell in the five juice bars he had all over town. With my confidence on the rise, I called up my other health club accounts to let them know that their competitors were selling these bars and they should get in on the action. That was all it took for the orders to start coming. I went from selling a couple dozen to a couple *hundred* dozen a week!

Within months I was getting calls from people around the country who had tried the bar when they were visiting Las Vegas. They wanted me to ship an order to their home. I'd probably put the cart a little ahead of the horse, because I wasn't even set up to take credit cards, nor did I have an account with UPS. I explained this to the customers, and most of them were so understanding they just mailed me a check and then I'd ship them the bars.

Once I was in most of the gyms around town, I took samples of the bars over to Wild Oats Market (a store that was later bought out by Whole Foods). I knew that they bought a lot of their bakery goods locally, and I figured that my Oat Bars were a good, healthy fit for a store with the name Wild Oats. I used the same sales tactic with them as I had with the gyms.

"Your competition is selling these and they're going fast!"

Again, it worked. They placed an order for ten dozen. And once those sold out they placed an order for ten dozen more. Then the other Wild Oats in town got wind of it and they placed an order. I was cruising. Just a year into the business I could sense I was on the cusp of something huge. The problem was my operation was still pretty inefficient, and I couldn't handle all these orders myself. So I hired a baker, a guy named Jorge, who seemed to have a real good attitude and an even better work ethic. Between his wages and what I paid an older couple I brought on to help out, I was pretty much kissing any profit margin away, but my sales were up. That was the main thing. All the rest would follow. I was sure of it.

CHAPTER 10

EVEN THOUGH I WAS broke, I decided to take a vacation. Actually, it was more of a family trip than a vacation. A friend of the family was getting married in Mexico. The woman, Brenda, was a close friend of my sister, Barbara. They had met one another in Orizaba, Vera Cruz, where Barbara lived and worked for several years. Brenda later attended Boston University and lived at my parents' house, and over the years our families had grown pretty close, so she invited the whole crew down for the wedding. My sister and I were talking on the phone before we left and I joked around with her, "You gonna help me find a wife down there?"

Well, I almost didn't make it. There was some misunderstanding at the airport regarding what documents I needed in order to be allowed into the country. I had called ahead, but they didn't give me accurate information. Once I got to the airport I learned I couldn't go without a passport. I explained that that was not the information I'd been given. After talking to a few people, they finally let me sign an affidavit swearing my own identity and go on my way.

I arrived in Mexico City at the same time as my sister and her husband, and we met up with my sister's friend Itzel and her brother, Gustavo, who were there to drive us five hours south to Orizaba. No sooner had we left the airport than the local police stopped us. They were a couple of burly, rough-looking guys—the kind you didn't want to mess with. They must have noticed that the two cars we were riding in had out-of-state plates. They probably saw us as their chance to make some quick cash, particularly when they discovered Gustavo's driver's license had expired. They told us we weren't going anywhere until we paid them off.

Gustavo tried to talk his way out of it, I think. I wasn't really sure what was going on since I didn't speak any Spanish. All I really knew was that those guys were pretty scary looking.

After some back and forth, the talking stopped and Gustavo went through his wallet. He handed the policemen some bills. It was the equivalent, he later told me, of seventy U.S. dollars. Then they told him that he might be stopped by other cops along the way, and they gave him a password to tell those cops, just in case, so they'd know to let him—us—through.

The rest of the drive went without incident and we arrived at Itzel's house for some refreshments. My sister and Itzel had arranged ahead of time for all of us to stay at different houses with family and friends so we wouldn't have to pay for hotel rooms. My parents had already been there for several days and were staying at Brenda's house with her and her parents. Barbara and her husband were going to stay at Itzel's house, and they had arranged for me to stay at Itzel's mother's house, where both her mother and her sister, Monica, lived.

When I arrived I had every intention of staying at a hotel. It was 1997 and I hadn't been on any kind of vacation since, well, since I was thirteen years old and in Peru. I wanted to relax and enjoy the modern comforts, like air-conditioning and cable television. I told them my plan, but then Monica came over to her sister's house and in that instant everything changed. Just looking at her was enough to change my mind about the hotel.

She was drop-dead gorgeous. Her skin was this beautiful dark tan color and her body was like a work of art. She looked young, may nineteen or twenty. She was perfect. That was my first thought; my second thought was there was no way she'd ever go for me.

So, Monica took me back to her house. She couldn't speak much English and I didn't know a word of Spanish, which made our conversation pretty slow and clumsy. But sometimes you don't need conversation.

Over the next week we spent almost all our time together, and with the help of a dictionary we got to know one another as best we could. I learned she was actually twenty-eight, recently divorced, and a high school and college teacher. I also found out that she was a runner, which accounted for her kick-ass body.

I was too insecure to actually make a move. Even though she seemed interested in everything I had to say, and even though she wanted to be around me all the time, I didn't think she liked me. Not like that, anyway. No woman who looked that good would ever, ever be interested in me romantically, so I figured she was just being nice, friendly. It was part of the culture.

The thing is I hadn't been very lucky in relationships with women in the past. I'd had some one-night stands, but nothing more involved than that. Since culinary school I'd put a lot of weight back on, and it was still a huge obstacle, mentally and physically. Why would any woman in her right mind want to be with a fat guy like me? I mean, the day we attended the wedding I sat down on a plastic chair and it actually broke.

But it didn't seem to faze her, so I started to get a little bolder. She gave me a tour around town that included the gym where she worked out. I asked her, partly in broken Spanish, partly in broken English, what she did to get in shape. Specifically I asked her about different abdomen exercises, hoping that it would convince her to show me more of her body.

"I want to see your stomach," I told her. She blushed and just kind of laughed it off, though, too embarrassed to show me anything.

Over and over again I thought about kissing her, and one night I almost did. We were out for dinner, and she looked so beautiful, wearing this sexy yellow dress. I couldn't stop thinking about kissing her all the way through our meal—and then I lost my nerve.

When the week was over and it was time for me to leave, I had it all planned out. This time I was going to kiss her, for real. I had to let this woman know my feelings. I would be kicking myself for the rest of my life if I went back to Vegas without at least trying.

So there we were, saying good-bye to one another after this incredible week, gazing into each other's eyes for what could be the last time, and I did it. I went in to kiss the woman I was falling in love with . . . And she turned her head. I felt completely humiliated.

When I got back to Mr. Muffin I figured the whole Monica situation was hopeless and I threw myself into work. We had talked about her coming to visit me, and I told her I would call her, but after that farewell I pushed it out of my mind. I felt rejected, and it confirmed what I'd suspected all along: She was just being nice and didn't really want to see or hear from me again. I mean she had refused my kiss! I was better off just focusing on my company and forging ahead.

But I couldn't get her out of my mind. She put some kind of spell on me or something. I'd never felt this way about anyone, and I knew I'd be an idiot to just let her go. So I called her up and was immediately glad I did. She told me, in her broken English, that she still wanted to come visit me, and I told her I hoped that she would. Then she purchased a plane ticket and told me she'd be staying for two weeks. She asked if I needed anything from Mexico, and I asked if she could bring some coffee and vanilla for the muffin shop. I'd bought some when I was down there and my supply was already dwindling.

I couldn't wait to see her and show her around, but I had some mixed feelings about it. Even though our backgrounds were so different and our languages were so different, I felt like we really connected. At the same time, I was also feeling frustrated, because in my thick head I figured she was just coming to visit because she'd never been to Las Vegas and she wanted to find something new and different to do on her summer break. Now that she knew me, she had a free place to stay and an excuse to check out the town. The notion that she was actually coming here to spend time with me didn't even cross my mind.

♦

I got to McCarran International Airport on August 8 to pick up Monica. I waited and waited but she was nowhere in sight. I started getting impatient, which quickly turned to worry. According to the monitors the flight had landed nearly an hour and a half prior. Could she have missed her flight? What could have happened?

Then I saw her. She was walking toward me, tan, trim, and beautiful, and I could feel that same familiar feeling I had in Mexico. Deep down, I knew I was falling in love with this woman. When she reached me we just stood there, awkwardly, grinning. Neither of us moved in for a hug.

She looked happy and a little bit frazzled. It turned out she'd been through the ringer. She explained that she was late because Customs stopped her and gave her a hard time about the coffee she had brought me. Apparently, coffee was used to smuggle drugs—and as a former drug dealer I didn't even know this—so they tore apart every single part of her luggage, right down to her underwear. No wonder she looked relieved to see me.

I took her on a quick tour of the town, driving down the famous Las Vegas Strip. As we passed the gigantic casinos and flashing neon signs, I pointed out some of the highlights, like Caesars Palace, Luxor, Excalibur. I tried to be a good tour guide and tell her about the different properties, but with the language barrier I wasn't sure how much she could really understand. By then, we'd come to rely so heavily on our English-Spanish dictionary that it was worn and wrinkled from use. But it didn't take any dictionary to know from her wide eyes and her smile that she was impressed.

Then I took her to my house. I got her settled into one of my spare rooms and explained as best I could that I had to work the next couple of days, but that she should make herself at home, relax, use the pool, whatever she wanted. She seemed okay with that.

Over the course of the next two weeks, I did my best to woo her. I cooked her dinner, made her laugh, took her out. We went shopping at the Forum Shops at Caesars Palace—mostly window-shopping and people-watching. As we walked past one jeweler's, I said to Monica, "One day, when I have money, I'm going to walk in there with a big wad of cash and buy a Rolex."

I took Monica to dinner at the Top of the World Restaurant, a revolving restaurant that sits at the top of the Stratosphere Hotel and Casino, looking down on the lights of the Strip. It's a real romantic spot, real intimate. Afterward we stood on the Stratosphere's observation deck nearly nine hundred feet above the city. I was so swept away by her beauty that I thought to myself, *Now is the time.* With my heart racing a mile a minute, I bent over and kissed her on the lips . . .

She kissed me back. Again and again, she kissed me back. I don't know if I'd ever been happier.

◆

I wanted Monica to see more than just Las Vegas, so I took her to Disneyland in Anaheim, California. It was spur of the moment, and all the hotels were booked with the exception of Portofino, a luxurious resort overlooking a marina. They offered me a room rate of $250 a night. That was sometimes more than I cleared in an entire week, but I knew it would mean spending the night with Monica, and it would be completely worth it.

Over the next three days we traveled around playing tourist, and in the middle of the dolphin show at Universal Studios, I pulled out my dictionary and told Monica that I wished she would stay in Las Vegas.

"I love you," I told her.

Her face lit up.

"I love you, too," she said, and she agreed to stay with me.

I was flooded with emotions. Monica was the love of my life, but it was more than that. Before I got sober, the women I was with were addicts who used me for drugs. I never could have gotten a woman of Monica's caliber to look my way. The thought of living together made me feel good about everything I'd done up to then. All at once I felt energized, happy—and terrified. I was afraid that once she saw all of my living habits she'd change her mind.

She knew about my past, and she accepted it. Her family had actually told her about my history of addiction before we'd met (and even warned her away from me because of it, I came to find out). But it was the little things I worried about. We were both adults, and we were both set in our ways. As a bachelor, I wasn't the cleanest person in the world, and I wasn't really used to compromising.

Over the weekend we'd already gotten in our first tiff after she used my razor to shave her legs. I told her that wasn't good for my razor and asked her not to do it again. She gave me this angry stare. I knew she had a fiery personality, but that was unlike anything I'd ever seen from her.

After we drove back to Vegas it was like we had to start over with one another romantically. I'm not sure what it was. Maybe we could both feel the weight of this decision and the impending change to our lives. Both of us were nervous, unsure, quiet. I led her into my bedroom and we both awkwardly sat on the edge of my bed, not sure what the next step would be.

"Are you going to sleep here?" I asked, hopeful.

She was coy for a moment, and then smiled shyly and said, "Yes."

We leaned toward one another and kissed. The shifting of our combined weight was just enough to flip the mattress off the bed onto the floor. We both cracked up, and all of the nervousness disappeared. It was just what we needed.

CHAPTER 11

FAMILY HAD ALWAYS BEEN very important to Monica, and to the Mexican culture in general. So getting her to agree to move to Las Vegas to live with me turned out to be the easy part. The hard part? Her mom and dad.

The tears came almost immediately when she called her mom. I sat there, watching her try to explain her decision while also trying to get control over her tears. Even though I couldn't understand what they were saying, I could tell that it was very difficult for her. It must have seemed like such a ridiculous notion to her parents. Think about it: she was the baby in this Mexican Catholic family and she was telling her mom that she was leaving two jobs and her entire world to move in with a Jewish man she'd just met—in Las Vegas. As I watched her cry, I felt helpless. I was afraid she would change her mind.

When her father got on the line, the tone of the phone call changed.

"It's moving too fast," he told Monica. "You just met this man. Just come home and think about it."

When that didn't work, he got more personal.

"He'll just grow tired of you after a while," he said, and around that time she really started getting upset. Suddenly, she hung up. I looked at her and she could see the question on my face.

"He asked if we're sleeping together," she told me. "I pretended something was wrong with the phone and hung up."

Once again, I knew that this was the girl for me.

♦

I took Monica hostage at the muffin shop. She was in Las Vegas, she was a hard worker and didn't have a job, and I really needed help. She worked on the retail side, and her Spanish language skills came in handy helping me communicate with my employees. I was able to eliminate another position, so she was also helping me cut back on costs.

What I really needed at the shop was some kind of machine to help me get the job done. I was spending too much time doing the tedious tasks, like wrapping the bars, and I figured if I could find some kind of automated system that would do that for me, it would really take me to the next level. I didn't have the money to buy one, but that had never stopped me before.

I looked around and found a company that refurbished used packaging machines and found one that would wrap up my items, no problem, so long as I was willing to pony up $11,000.

Eleven THOUSAND dollars! To a broke guy who had just sunk all his savings and then some into a business, that was all the money in the world. I looked around again at my options and I found a company that leased equipment. They were basically middlemen: they would buy the equipment outright, I would make payments to them, and they could charge me an interest rate that a loan shark would be proud of—40 percent. Since I'd pretty much maxed my credit cards and didn't qualify for a home equity or personal loan, it was really my only choice.

On top of that, the guy who owned the machine was giving me the runaround. He'd put me off for months before finally inviting me to fly to Northern California to try out the machine. So Jorge and I flew up there, only to discover the equipment we were about to lease was being stored in some guy's barn. Not only that, it didn't even work. The guy shrugged it off, saying it was just having some mechanical issues, and he swore that if I agreed to lease it he'd have it ready in the allotted time. I was a pretty optimistic guy, and it was the best price I could find on this type of machine, so I went for it. I signed on the dotted line and waited for them to fix it up and deliver it.

Back at the shop, we were all putting in all kinds of crazy hours, working sometimes more than ten hours a day, seven days a week, just to keep on top of our orders. I hoped the machine would help lighten our load, but I knew it wasn't the be-all end-all solution. So when Jorge told me he needed help, I believed him. He said he wanted to bring his father to Vegas and asked if I would be willing to give him a job. I liked the idea of bringing an extra pair of hands into the mix, and I was a trusting guy, willing to help out my workers, so I agreed to it. I figured it was a win-win situation.

It wasn't the first time I'd been wrong. Jorge's father, Pablo, arrived the next week. He did a decent job helping out with the baking and the wrapping, but once he was in the kitchen, I began seeing a personality shift in Jorge. The son became more demanding, asking for more money and fewer hours. His father started pulling the same thing, and I suddenly understood why many companies have a policy against hiring family members. I was in a tough spot. They knew that I relied heavily on both of them and thought that gave them the upper hand. As much as they pushed, I pulled. I refused to give in. I was curious to see how far they'd really take this.

When the packaging machine finally arrived, it seemed like the great equalizer, at least for a little while. None of us had a clue what to do with it. First of all, it was this giant, heavy, rectangular machine that weighed somewhere between 600 and 700 hundred pounds. It was so big that it wouldn't even fit though the front door, so we actually had to take the door off and use a dolly to push the monstrous machine inside. That was just the beginning.

The company sent a guy down to show us how to use it. Man, it was complicated. The machine was made in the 1970s, and everything about it needed constant adjusting. I almost started to kick it more than a few times. All in all, it was a total nightmare. I'd expected to turn on this automatic wonder that did all the work for us. What I got was just about the opposite, and if used incorrectly it crushed my muffins. I began wondering if I'd made a mistake.

Regardless, I was stuck. I'd signed a three-year lease for the thing, so I had to make it work. Jorge and his father complained nonstop and were pretty peeved that their lives just got more difficult. I was okay with that, though. They had already been making my life more difficult.

It was always something. My frustration was compounded by the fact that Monica and I were dedicating pretty much all of our time to the muffin shop, yet by the end of the week, we didn't even have $100 between the two of us. I started to wonder, for the first time, was this whole thing really worth it? I'd always had faith that I'd be successful in life. But was this the key to it?

Never one to quit, I figured it was time for an overhaul of my business plan. Looking it over, it was pretty clear what I needed to do. I needed to go big. A hundred boxes here and a hundred boxes there just weren't cutting it. I needed orders, and I needed them in the thousands.

I found out the name of the national director of purchasing for Wild Oats Markets, and I sent him a letter. I told him how well the bars were doing at the local level, and I included a bunch of samples. A few days later, he called me when I was in the middle of my delivery route. I was in a sour mood because I'd sold a total of five muffins for $10 for the entire day. His call was exactly what I needed.

He told me he enjoyed the samples, but that Wild Oats outsourced their distribution. He gave me the phone number of a guy named Matt, who worked for a company called DPI, one of the main distributors. I got a hold of Matt and he told me he was in the process of leaving DPI to start his own business. He said he'd help me get the bars in the stores, but there was a catch—as my broker, he'd get a 5 percent commission.

If I'd learned one thing in the business world it was that everyone had his or her hand out. And since I was a newcomer, they expected that their hand would fill up pretty quickly and easily. Even though I barely had two coins to rub together, I wanted the opportunity he was offering. I decided to work him just like he was working me. I told him I'd be happy to do business with him but my minimum order was one pallet. That's a hundred cases of forty-eight bars—forty-eight hundred bars. It was nearly six times the size of the biggest order I'd made in the past.

He agreed.

I had a smile stretched across my face that wouldn't go away when I went and told Monica. The purchase order was nearly $2,000 more than any check I'd ever seen in my life.

Then reality set in. I needed to get to work! I had to admit, as soon as the words "one pallet" had left my mouth, I didn't have a clue as to how I was going to ship them, store them, or even make them. As I've mentioned, even one batch of bars was a long, involved process. Now I was faced with nearly five thousand bars!

I had to heat up the honey and liquid sugar at my house because I didn't have a tabletop stove at the muffin shop. So I went home, filled two lobster pots with water, liquid sugar, and honey and brought the mixture to boil and, in the process, covered the entire kitchen in a sticky sheen, which annoyed Monica no end. Then I loaded the buckets into the back of my truck and drove them half an hour across town to the muffin shop. Once I was there, I poured the liquid into that ancient mixer along with oats and oat flour, raisins, and cocoa. The mixer had enough room for only twenty-four bars, and three batches would fill a sheet pan. It took about an hour to make a hundred bars, and then I'd set them on baking racks to dry for about four hours, after which they were frozen. And then the process would start all over again. And again. And again.

It took five days of working almost nonstop. Then we packed them into large boxes and called a refrigerator truck to deliver them to Colorado. I pictured them arriving at the Wild Oats headquarters and selling like gangbusters. Everyone would want them, everyone would order more, and I'd soon be making the big bucks. Right?

Well, I didn't hear anything about them for weeks. After about a month and a half I called Matt to ask how they were doing. I was pretty shocked when he told me that hardly any stores had ordered any, and they were mostly all still sitting right there in Colorado, in the warehouse. Apparently, getting the distributor to order and the stores to order were two entirely different things. I wished I had known that earlier.

My stomach dropped as I pictured my bars sitting there. I asked what we could do, and he said he was going to send one case of each flavor to a bunch of different stores, unsolicited. That way, the distributor's inventory would be depleted and the bars would at least be in the right hands. I decided to help him out and sent signs and baskets to each of the stores where he was sending the bars. I figured it was a nice, helpful thing to do.

Then I sat back, again, and waited for the orders to start rolling in. The phone started ringing within a couple days, but it wasn't at all what I had expected. There was a backlash. An angry, peeved backlash from storeowners who demanded to know why they had received products that they didn't order.

I tried to calm them down by explaining that it was a new product approved by the corporate purchasing department.

"The bars sell very well in the current stores they're in," I explained. "And I would be happy to support you in any way you'd like with promotional materials."

It was enough to convince most of the managers to give the bars a try, and in most cases, they were a hit. From there the distributor's orders came in regularly about every six weeks, one pallet at a time.

Believe it or not, the sudden increase in sales didn't solve all of my financial issues like I'd hoped it would. Don't get me wrong; I was extremely happy to be making sales outside my little Las Vegas circle of stores. But I was somehow still chasing after a profit, struggling to pay for all the labor, materials, and machinery. Every six weeks or so I was clearing only about $1,200. So I just kept pounding away. I continued stockpiling orders with Wild Oats. I approached vending machine companies and had some success. I tried anything and everything I could, and the harder I tried the more orders I got, but I just kept waiting for the influx of cash to follow.

As Jorge and his dad watched the increase in business, they assumed I was bringing in a lot more money than I actually was, and they wanted a slice of the action. They waited until we were in the middle of filling a giant order for a vending machine company, and they gave me an ultimatum: raise their pay by 60 percent or the mixer would go off.

I agreed with them, I told them they had a deal. At the same time, I started plotting how I would replace them. As soon as we filled that order I brought in a new guy named Alejandro and fired those two. That's what happens when you deal in ultimatums.

♦

Even though I was still struggling financially, I was happier than I'd ever been. Monica had been living with me for about six months, and we were completely in love. One night, I decided to ask her to marry me.

She laughed.

That began a series of proposals, to the point of ridiculousness. I had no doubt that she was the woman with whom I wanted to spend the rest of my life. I knew she felt the same way, but because she had been married and divorced once before, she had reservations. Month after month I popped the question. Day after day, night after night, she laughed it off.

Finally, after about three months of rejection, we were lying in bed and I asked her for the hundredth time, "Will you marry me?"

She smiled and said the word I'd been waiting for: "Yes."

A couple of weeks later our families flew in for the wedding. We'd both planned on scaling back our work hours and really enjoying a week of celebration.

Then Alejandro quit. He told me that he had a medical problem and was returning to Mexico. I had no choice but to spend eighteen hours a day at the bakery, trying to make everything we needed on my own. I hardly had a chance to see our families, and they weren't subtle about how upset they were.

"Why don't you just close for a few days?" they asked.

I tried to explain that we couldn't do that—it was our livelihood, and even in a good week we were struggling. No matter what I said, they thought we were ignoring them. It was a quick lesson in Reality 101. For one thing, people who had worked at a job their whole life couldn't begin to understand the rigors and demands of working for yourself. Second, your employees would never care about the business like you did, and they couldn't care less if they inconvenienced you in any way.

Regardless of the week's rocky start, Monica and I got married at the Flamingo Hotel and Casino, which had been made famous by its mobster owner, Bugsy Siegel. About fifty people attended the ceremony, but my eyes were only on Monica. She looked absolutely stunning, and I still couldn't quite understand why she ever agreed to marry a guy like me.

CHAPTER 12

I BEGAN TRAVELING TO California to try to broaden the market for my bars. During my travels I heard about a distributor that specialized in frozen products for businesses like juice bars. I contacted them and was told that if I participated in their tradeshow, they'd take my bars on consignment. It sounded like a good opportunity to expand the market.

Problem was, I'd need to make five thousand bars for the trade show, and as always, I had nothing. No credit, no money, nothing. So I swallowed my pride and asked my father if I could borrow $10,000. Thankfully, he agreed. I think that he was glad I was doing something positive with the money for a change.

I used the loan to cover my immediate expenses—like a new, larger mixer, and the tradeshow fee—and I registered for a UPC number. That's the barcode number that is associated with your product and placed on price tags so retailers can just scan it into the computer. I figured if I were really going to go big, I'd need that number down the line, so I went ahead and paid the $600.

That show really helped me develop a more solid business vision. I hadn't expected to be so swept away in the spirit of the health food products. I had always thought that these bars could be my ticket, and that show confirmed it. I met a ton of people, and they all had positive things to say about the bars. Looking around at the dedicated following, I realized that this was really the best way to make money—it wasn't muffins, brownies, or cookies. That was when I made the executive decision to focus solely on selling bars. I was ready to start turning a profit and this was the best way. I just knew it.

It was a huge risk, but I didn't care. Even though muffins were bringing in 30 to 40 percent of my revenue, I could just feel that this was the right direction. I also had a hunch that if I didn't take a risk right then I could be struggling for the rest of my life. If I knew one thing, it was that there was never a perfect time to do anything. *If you feel strongly about something, you must throw caution to the wind, bury your fears, and go for it*, I said to myself. I had started with nothing; if I failed, I'd just be back where I started. I could always go back to driving a cab and give it another go. So I gave all of my customers two weeks' notice, and I closed Mr. Muffin in its retail capacity and used the bakery exclusively to make the bars.

Monica and I started making trips to Los Angeles every weekend to take care of business. It was a pretty rough way to end a sixty- to eighty-hour workweek. We would leave Las Vegas after having spent the whole day, since dawn, in the shop on Thursday. During the four-hour drive to LA, we were often so exhausted that we would pull into a rest stop and sleep until one of us had the energy to drive the rest of the way. Then on Friday we would travel around to five or six stores picking up the supplies we couldn't get in Vegas. The rest of the weekend we would hand out samples at different juice bars and nutrition stores, and Sunday we drove home and went straight to the bakery to package bars for Monday's shipments.

With all that work and nothing to show for it, Monica was getting frustrated. She was a good worker, but she hadn't exactly dreamed of being a laborer. I was following a vision and a goal, whereas she was pretty much there to help me out and be supportive.

One time we were at the shop all night long trying to get the packaging to seal. We drove home at six o'clock in the morning and crawled into bed, exhausted. As I was drifting off, I heard Monica crying.

"Can't you just quit?" she pleaded with me. "Can't you just get a real job?"

I promised her that if we just kept at it, one day we'd have a lot of money. I told her she just had to believe in me. But even as I said it, even as I believed in it myself, I wanted a better life for us.

By the time our first anniversary rolled around, I was still broke. I could hardly pay our cable bill, much less think about getting Monica an extravagant gift or taking her out for a nice meal. But I wanted to do something for her. She'd been there through a lot of tough times, and I knew for a fact I wouldn't be where I was without her.

I went to a coin dealer and pulled out the gold coin necklace I wore around my neck. It was a symbol of my sobriety and had been one of the first things I bought after I got sober and started making money. It was a one-ounce gold American Eagle coin, and the guy gave me $600 for it. It was just enough to take Monica out to dinner and a show. It may not have made up for all the tears and sadness, and the fact that she was living a life she never really bargained for, but it was still something.

Or at least, I thought it was. I got home and told Monica I was taking her to dinner and then to see "Crazy Girls," a dance show at the Riviera Hotel Casino. She looked at me, surprised. She knew we couldn't afford that kind of thing.

"Where did you get the money?" she demanded.

I told her.

"What's next, the TV?" she asked, sobbing.

It made me feel even worse. But I talked to her, calmed her down, and explained that this was only temporary and things would get better. They *would* get better.

A few weeks later, things did start coming together. The frozen distributor's sales were growing, and Wild Oats' orders were coming in more frequently. It was a fast enough pace to warrant hiring some help to keep up. I brought on my brother Eric, who had just gotten a job in Vegas as a firefighter a few weeks earlier, along with some other people to help take some of the strain off Monica and me. Looking around, it felt good to actually see an assembly line in motion.

Then we found out Monica was pregnant. We were floored.

We had talked about kids and agreed that we didn't want them. I was terrified of becoming like my father and never wanted to do that to a child. The easy and obvious solution was to just avoid conceiving. Monica always acted like she felt the same way.

When we found out she was pregnant, I wasn't exactly thrilled with it. I kept my feelings to myself, but I think she knew. Barely making enough money to support ourselves, I didn't know how we were going to support a baby. Plus, I didn't know how the drugs and alcohol had affected my reproductive system. The whole idea raised all kinds of emotions in me, and I couldn't help but think of that baby as a burden. It sounds cruel, but it was true.

We didn't have any health insurance, so we signed up for a program called Baby Your Baby, which helped with prenatal and birth expenses. The program also taught you about parenthood and gave you some of the basics you'd need when the baby came along. About two months into the pregnancy Monica started bleeding. I took her to the emergency room, where we found out she'd lost the baby.

My wife became horribly depressed. She started crying all the time and didn't want to get out of bed. Through her tears she told me that she'd had a miscarriage with her previous husband as well, and I realized that maybe she hadn't been quite so truthful about not wanting children. I comforted her as best I could and told her not to worry, we'd try again. I hated seeing her in pain. I figured if she wanted a baby this badly then that's what we would do. I would just have to deal with my baggage and overcome what seemed to be my family curse. I would be a good father.

◆

In the midst of the emotions that Monica and I were dealing with, I got an uplifting phone call. It was from a guy named James who, it turned out, was a customer of mine and also happened to be a local sports nutrition distributor. He told me that he worked out at the local

Gold's Gym, and every day he bought one of the Oat Bars after his workout. Over the last couple of years, he'd watched as the sales of the bars went up, and he told me he was actually interested in distributing them.

So I met with James and two of his associates at a TGI Friday's, and he told me about how they used to own a protein drink manufacturing company, which they'd sold. He'd recently started a company called Sports Nutrition and thought that my Oat Bars could be the next big thing. He'd kept in contact with distributors from the days of their protein drink, and they also had a direct-to-consumer supplement company that they ran.

They wanted to buy the bars from me, package them in a private label that they would design, and then resell them to their network. But the only way they'd do it, James told me, was if I started making a peanut-butter-flavored bar. That was the best-selling flavor in sports nutrition food by a two-to-one margin. If I agreed to do that and to work with them, James told me he was pretty sure he could mark up the price I'd been getting by about a third, from 50 cents to 75 cents, easy, and sell two to three pallets a week. That translated to about fifteen thousand bars, grossing $7,500.

It was a deal. As James and his colleagues set about their new package design, I immersed myself in experimenting with peanut butter flavors. I had to create a flavor that wasn't too strong, but not too weak, and it had to be natural. I called around to different manufacturers and got nearly thirty samples to begin with, but I quickly discovered that none of them seemed right. After trying more than a hundred different recipes, the essence was still off. I added peanut flour, and then I added a pure form of peanut oil. I mixed up a bunch of batches and finally, finally found a combination I was happy with.

I shared samples with James and the guys, and they were happy with it too. They showed me some of the designs they'd come up with for the packaging, and they looked pretty good—a lot better, actually, than the one I'd been using. So, with those steps out of the way, we were ready to start filling up the pallets. I contacted Wild Oats to tell them about the new peanut-butter-flavored bar, and they agreed to add the flavor to their inventory too.

Now that I was working with James I decided it was time to make some changes in other places. I cut ties with the frozen distributor. While I'd had some luck with them, I felt like our relationship had reached the end of its shelf life. With that option eliminated, I started thinking about ways to generate sales. My clients at the time were pretty lopsided in the direction of the sports nutrition distributors, and I wanted to diversify. I contacted a marketing company that specialized in the natural food business. Two women and two men ran A Marketing, and they managed a network of brokers working exclusively in the natural food industry. Those brokers called on distributors, retail chain stores, and mom-and-pop health food stores to market natural products. They told me that in exchange for their services they received a percentage of sales—usually 5 percent—and operated on retainer, with a minimum fee of $1,600 a month, but they could double that for a national roll out. I decided to give them a try. I'd finally reached a point where I was making enough money to support Monica and me, but I wanted to make sure we had a financial cushion.

I couldn't afford the $3,200 they charged to take distribution national, so Grace, my contact at A Marketing, told me they could focus on three regions for $1,600 a month. I agreed, thinking it would more than pay for itself in sales.

Meanwhile, Sports Nutrition sales were taking off. The faster they sold them, the faster I made them. I was cranking out so many bars that I ran out of cooler space at my bakery. Rather than buy a new cooler I walked next door and talked to my neighbor, who ran an Indian take-out chicken restaurant. The owner's English wasn't great, but I explained my dilemma to her and asked if I could rent a portion of her refrigerator to store my bars. She was eager to do it.

"I like to make business," she said to me.

"I like to make business too," I smiled, and we shook hands.

From then on, Monica and I started taking stacks and stacks of bars over to her walk-in. We'd walk into the six-hundred-square-foot cooler, stride past the raw, marinating chickens and vegetables, and take up about two hundred square feet with our bars and pay her $150 a month. I think it annoyed the day-to-day workers, but it sure helped me out of a jam.

The cooler was just the first indication that I was going to need to expand soon. By now I had four people who came in to mix and roll out the bars by hand in the morning and then three more came in to score, cut, flip, separate, package, label, stamp, box, and freeze the bars in the afternoon. It was a lot of people and a lot of work in a very small space. I started looking for ways that I could get higher productivity with less labor. If I could find a machine to make the bars and a machine to label the bars I could streamline the whole process. So I called my old packaging machine pal and asked him if he could help.

He told me that his company had a machine designed to work with bread dough, and it would work just as well with my bars, mixing, rolling and then cutting them. I loved the sound of it. Then he told me the price: $40,000. I was stunned all right, but if the equipment could do what they said it could do—make one hundred pieces a minute—I wanted it. I figured I'd find a way to get it, just like I always had.

Monica and I talked about our options, financially. Business was good, but still not that good. A home equity line of credit was out of the question. I didn't make enough verifiable income to satisfy the bank's requirements. Our families weren't interested in helping. I asked James about investing, but he wasn't game unless I was willing to hand over a larger stake in the company. The best option was to lease the machine.

The day before I was going to sign the lease, I had begun calling around to a few different businesses in search of some cooling racks. As luck would have it, I ended up calling a company in the Cleveland area. I was talking to the salesman, Gino, about the manufacturing machine I was going to lease. He had a machine that was $15,000 cheaper than the one I was looking at. He said he was about to sell it to another customer, but if I could get there pronto I could try it out.

I booked a flight on a red-eye and packed up all the ingredients I'd need to make the bars. I loaded up the dry ingredients in bags and put the liquid ingredients into a bunch of water bottles. I flew into Cleveland, and at 8:00 a.m. Gino was there to pick me up from the airport and drive me the twenty-five miles to his shop.

When we got to the store, I went to get my stuff out of the backseat of his car and a wave of panic passed over me. His backseat was covered in gooey, sticky stuff. My water bottles must have gotten messed up by the pressure of flying, because now they had leaked all over the velour seat coverings of Gino's car. It was awful. He took a bunch of handkerchiefs and wiped at it, but it didn't do much good. I just stood there, embarrassed, not sure what to do.

We went into the store, and fortunately, I still had enough liquid left to make a small batch of my bars. The equipment wasn't perfect, but the important thing was that it was better than the way I was running things. I decided to go with this cheaper model. I figured that way I'd still have $15,000 in financing to buy a labeling machine, and once I got that, I'd practically have the entire process automated. I returned to Las Vegas confident I'd made the right decision.

Gino told me it would take about a month before the machine would be delivered. While I was waiting for it to come in I got a call from a guy named Sam, who identified himself as a venture capitalist. He'd been traveling in California and tried one of my Oat Bars. He told me he enjoyed the bar and was interested in possibly investing in the company. He might as well have dangled a steak in front of a starving man. I agreed to meet with him for dinner.

Sam was a blonde, good-looking, fit guy, somewhere in his late thirties, early forties. I could tell immediately that he took care of himself. He came from outside Detroit and had made his money designing magnesium parts for the auto industry. He was an engineer by trade, he said, but he was into fitness and wanted to put his money into something related to the fitness industry.

I told him more about my company and my background. I also mentioned the machine I was buying in Ohio, and he said that when I went to pick up the machine he'd be interested in driving down from Michigan and talking further. I kind of took it with a grain of salt. I was always skeptical about people who were offering to invest money. There were a whole lot of talkers out there.

But a few weeks later, when Monica and I flew to Ohio, Sam was still interested, and we met again for dinner. This time Monica came along, and she liked Sam immediately. He felt the same way. In fact, when she left the table, Sam leaned over and told me, "I wish I were lucky enough to meet a woman like Monica."

The way he said it was genuine, and I felt really proud and lucky to have her in my life. I guess it also warmed me up to him a little bit more. I told him more about my future plans for the company, and about what I'd done so far, and he seemed to be more comfortable with the business and with me, as a person. He implied that he might be willing to invest up to $100,000. I tried to keep a poker face, but I also didn't want to seem aloof. That was money I could really use. When we parted ways, I got the sense I'd be hearing from Sam soon.

The next day Monica and I went to check out the machine, but it wasn't working right. It was cutting bars, but not very well, and they weren't in the right shape. Gino assured me that it just needed a few adjustments and a better set of cutting wheels.

"Take it home," he told me, and promised to send a guy out to work on it in the field. I wasn't thrilled with the scenario, but I didn't feel like I had much of a choice. So I took the semi-functioning machine back to Vegas.

A few days after we got home we learned that Monica was pregnant.

CHAPTER 13

THIS TIME IT WASN'T exactly a surprise. Monica had never quite gotten over the miscarriage and really wanted to have a baby, so we'd been trying. Still, it was kind of a surprise for a guy who still wasn't convinced that the whole idea of reproduction was for him. My mind went back to my father and his father before him—the abuse, the coldness, the disappointment. When I thought of fatherhood, those words—and the feelings they evoked—were what came to mind.

But I was conflicted. The more I thought about it the more I realized how much I really, really wanted to have a son, someone to carry on the family name. In some ways that feeling had always been there, but the pain from my upbringing buried it. I was beginning to realize that behind all of the hurtful memories there was a void. It was something that I thought having a kid of my own could fill.

About two months into the pregnancy Monica started bleeding. It was just like the previous time. We didn't say it, didn't say anything, but we each knew what the other was thinking. Since Monica had had two miscarriages already, she was terrified that she'd lost this one, and I was terrified of seeing her go through that kind of gut-wrenching pain and depression. As I drove her to the doctor I silently pleaded for the baby to be okay.

When we got to the hospital they performed some tests and then told us that the baby was okay, and Monica was okay too. We were both relieved, but still worried. Because of the bleeding and her history she was classified as a high-risk pregnancy, and the doctor put her on bed rest for the next seven months. It was a frightening prospect, but so much better than the alternative. Her mom flew in from Mexico to help out.

The bed rest was really tough on both of us. We were used to being together all the time. It had been that way almost since the day we met. So, even though we were still living in the same house, spending the days apart wasn't easy. Plus, Monica had become a really important part of the company. She knew how everything ran and was involved in almost all aspects of it, from the overall operations to communicating with the employees.

But I did the best I could. While Monica was at home nurturing one part of our future, I worked on the financial side. I was really keeping my fingers crossed that Sam would come through because I was sick of my credit card companies calling and harassing me about how much I owed.

When I finally heard from Sam, we talked a bit about the kind of deal we would enter into, if we were to enter into any kind of deal. He was considering investing about $300,000, and for that he wanted 20 percent of the company. I liked the idea of it, but then he asked me all kinds of questions and gave me a long list of things he wanted to see: financial reports like my profit and loss statements, balance sheets, income statements. He wanted to see my books and a business plan; I didn't have any of what he asked for.

I assumed I had pretty much lost my chances of getting that $300,000, and that Sam would quietly back off. When I didn't hear from him for a few weeks, I figured we were done.

Like always, I just kept my head down and my nose to the grindstone. My employees and I were having a hell of a time figuring out the new

manufacturing machine from Ohio. Whenever a technician or someone from the company worked with it, it was fine. Then, the moment
they left, parts started breaking or bars got cut all wrong—there was
always something, and it usually had something to do with operator
error. But the more I worked with it the easier it got, for the most part.
And when it didn't get easier—like with the label machine—sometimes
I just gave in. After trying countless times to get that machine to work,
I got sick of coming in every day and seeing my workers stick the labels
on by hand while the machine collected dust in the corner. I decided
it wasn't worth the fight, and if they wanted to do things the hard way,
I wasn't going to stop them—even though I still had to pay for the
machine's five-year lease.

♦

The more pieces of fancy equipment I bought, the more space I needed.
Not only were the machines getting bigger, their output was too. I started
thinking about finding a bigger space. The modest muffin shop was getting more and more cramped. The problem, however, was that I really
didn't have the financial records—or the finances, frankly—required to
lease a space. So I looked around for a place that was more lenient when
it came to tenants.

It took some searching but I found five thousand square feet of space
available in a new building. I couldn't afford it, but that had never
stopped me before. The owner didn't ask me for any financials, either. It
was like it was meant to be.

I arranged to pay for the build-out through the monthly rent over
the next five years. Add to that the cost of moving and the new $16,000
walk-in cooler I wanted to buy, and I was right back where I'd started:
broke, and unsure how I was going to make ends meet. I figured I would
try to sell Mr. Muffin to satisfy the remainder of my lease at the old spot,
and somehow the other things would work themselves out.

That's what I was thinking about when I got a call out of the blue
from Sam. He told me he was in town and asked to see my operation.

He went on to say that he was ready to invest, and he would be willing to sign a confidentiality agreement and wire $30,000 as a good-faith measure pending a deal that would be worked out.

That $30,000 might as well have been $1 million in my eyes, and I graciously accepted it. I ignored the subtle tugging at the back of my mind, telling me it may not be the wisest thing to do. Too busy to deal with any paperwork, we established a gentleman's agreement and moved forward. I figured if I needed to go back and draw up a legally binding document it wasn't a big deal, but for now I had the guy's word, and in my world that meant everything.

I don't think he knew how much he was saving my tail on this one, and I planned to keep those details to myself. Now, with Sam's backing, I'd be able to take on the lease and the other payments I needed to make. After all the stress over the financial situation of my business, I thought that with his help I'd finally be able to sleep at night.

I drew up a confidentiality agreement for Sam to sign and then, per his request, I took him to the muffin shop for a tour. I don't know if it was what he was expecting—after all, it was still just a tiny operation with some giant machines that even on a good day didn't all work. As I walked him through I watched his reaction, which was the opposite of impressed. Even though he didn't say anything I was certain Sam would run for cover. Like I said, it wasn't like we had any kind of written agreement.

Over the next few weeks, however, I was surprised to learn that Sam hadn't changed his mind. I guess he was satisfied enough by what he saw, because he kept wiring money in varying amounts into the bank account. I used it almost as fast as it came in.

♦

Back at home Monica was getting edgy. I was running around all day, handling all the business matters and putting in nearly eighty hours a week while she was confined to the bed. She had a lot of hours in which to realize exactly how much work I was putting into the store. Usually she was right there with me, but being away from it had a way of giving her perspective. Plus, with the baby coming along, her priorities were shifting. Mine still weren't.

We talked about possible names for the baby, and we both really liked Jacob. She wanted to start buying things and getting ready for his arrival, but I wouldn't let her do it. Jewish tradition holds that it's bad luck to buy anything before the child is born. And I wasn't about to tread on any kind of luck.

Especially not when everything seemed to be working in our favor at work. It took a few months, but before long my new space was done and I was ready to move in. I got a call from James, my old Sports Nutrition friend. He told me that he had sold his distributorship and was now on his own. His goal was to continue selling Oat Bars to his out-of-town distributors with his own private label. He asked if I had space available to rent out. At first it sounded like a good idea: it would be nice to have someone helping out with the rent. But then he started getting pushy. For some time already he'd been trying to get me to be his partner, and James presented me with a document saying as such. I'd always refused because he didn't want to contribute any money to the venture; he just wanted a part of the gains.

"You need my sales to stay in business," he insisted.

Well, I don't play hardball unless I'm the one who's pitching. So I told him about Sam. I figured if anything would motivate James to cough up some dough and become an investor it was a little bit of competition. Even with the influx of cash from Sam, I was in desperate need for some growth capital, and the only thing I had to raise funds with was my equity. Since James had just sold his company I knew he was in a pretty good position financially. I figured if he was interested I could sell a percentage of the company to him and still keep a controlling interest.

After informing him about the amount Sam was giving and how that got him a 20 percent share in the company, I asked James point-blank: "Would you be willing to put up the same? We could be three partners, or it could just be you and me, depending on how much you're willing to invest."

I swear when I told him that I thought he was going to cry. The bottom line was he still didn't want to part with a penny. It sounded like his past deals had all worked out so that he'd been allowed to put up minimal funds. Asking him for money was like telling him he had to give me one of his limbs. And no matter what I said, he wasn't willing to part with such things.

♦

Moving day came, and to save money I did it on my own. Sam actually flew in from Michigan to help me, and I have to say I was impressed. I didn't think a rich investor would do physical labor, but there he was, moving and carrying stuff as well as cleaning and vacuuming. I was pretty happy to have him as a part of the company. Getting his hands dirty showed some real dedication.

When we were all moved in, I started jumping through all of the necessary hoops with the Southern Nevada Health District. I had submitted my plans previously for approval, and they were in fact, approved, but I couldn't move forward until they signed off after doing a walk-through inspection. I called for an appointment and waited nervously for the inspector. I was effectively out of business until I got their final okay.

They came in, and it was exactly as I feared: I didn't get approved. They gave me a whole list of issues to deal with before they'd let me open: "Get rid of exposed insulation; get covering in the food prep area; paint the warehouse; get a mop sink; get an air curtain to place in the food prep area." I took issue with some of their requirements, but when it comes to a government agency, you can take issue with something until you're blue in the face and they still won't listen. Rather than drag my feet, I trudged through all of their red tape and made all of the requisite changes. One week later, and about $8,000 poorer, I had everything done. The inspector came back out, gave me his approval, and I was back in business.

CHAPTER 14

JANUARY 3, 2001, STARTED out pretty scary. Monica was bleeding, so we rushed to the hospital. Not this again.

After examining her they told us everything was okay—but she was in labor.

I was in the delivery room through it all, and it turned out to be one of the best days of my life. Seeing Jacob's birth was such a blessing. He was 7 pounds, seven ounces; he arrived at seven past seven o'clock in the morning; and he was my parents' seventh grandchild. In Vegas, it didn't get much luckier than that.

I cried the first moment I saw him. Life as I knew it changed. Jacob needed me, he needed Monica, and it was our obligation and duty to be there for him. His birth really made me reflect on my life. Up to that time I had only been responsible for me, and I hadn't done such a great job at that. But having two people dependent on me, I was determined to live up their expectations.

Monica's mom was at the hospital with her and Jacob, so I was able to go to the plant that afternoon. It was the first day of production after the Christmas and New Year's break, which meant that there was a lot of work to be done.

When I arrived at the plant, they were understaffed, so I filled in, weighing dry ingredients and doing whatever I could to help. But after just a couple of hours there, I was so exhausted—mentally, emotionally, and physically—that I actually decided to call off production. It was one of the only times I'd ever done that for personal reasons—hell, I hadn't even done it during the week of my wedding. But the birth of my first son sounded like a pretty damn good personal reason. The next day I went and picked up my family and took them home.

Monica's mother stuck around to help out with the baby, and I was truly grateful for that. Our house was a pretty stressful place for a while. I was worried about business and Monica was nervous about being a good mother. But we couldn't have been happier with Jacob. Having a baby turned out to be the most fulfilling thing we'd ever done.

♦

Still searching for that magic machine to seamlessly make my bars, Sam and I found an all-in-one setup that seemed to be the answer to our prayers. It would create the wrapper, wrap the bars, and seal them. I was so busy running the business and being a new dad that I decided to let Sam handle everything to do with the machine. It was his money, after all.

It took nearly seven months for this new machine to be built, which was more than anyone expected. By then, I'd come to accept that when new machinery was delivered there were going to be problems, no matter how good or how expensive the machine was. In fact, the more expensive it was the more room there was for problems.

And as our most expensive machine to date, this one was no different. It was a huge pain in the ass. On top of that, I questioned the costs that went into it every step of the way. Besides the machine itself we were looking at more than $100,000 to design a new package and buy a bunch of new boxes with our logo. My head was spinning from all the zeroes. Something just didn't seem right about it all. I was no expert, but I suspected we'd been had. Everyone Sam found seemed to overcharge us and tack on all kinds of ridiculous fees, and he just went along with them and paid it. It was going to take a lot of bars to recoup that investment. A lot of bars.

Once we had the machine in motion, Wild Oats put in a huge— huge—order: $50,000. It was a part of an ad promotion we were doing with them, selling the bars for a 15 percent discount in addition to an ad that ran in their flyers and was mailed out to homes across the country. To prepare for the onslaught, they had DPI, their distributor, stock their shelves with the bars. It was beginning to look like Sam and I would start to recoup some of the money we'd put into the business.

And then 9/11 happened.

Just like every other American, I will always remember where I was and what I was doing when I heard about the planes flying into the Twin Towers. I was attending the International Baking Industry Exposition at the Las Vegas Convention Center. I was there checking out yet another expensive machine to use to manufacture the bars. I'd spoken on the phone with the company reps who were from Massachusetts, and they invited me to the show to check it out. My hope was that I'd walk out of the show with that very machine.

I entered the enormous convention hall, and all around me, peoples' heads were tilted upward as they stared at the video monitors surrounding the hall. I joined them, watching as a plane flew into the building and smoke filled the screen. They showed it over and over and over again, and it wasn't just one plane, it was two. And it wasn't just any building; it was the World Trade Center in New York City.

It was surreal. Shocking. Incomprehensible. Everyone around me had pretty much the same stunned response. We all just stared at the monitors and watched the buildings crumble, the smoke rise, and the planes disappear.

At first the convention hall was silent. Crowds formed around each and every television and nobody said a word. As it sunk in, slowly, I started to hear people speak.

"How could this have happened?" It was the question on nearly everyone's lips. Then the cameras caught the people jumping from windows, high up in the towers, plunging in desperation to their death. I wanted to go home and just hug my family. Standing there in that convention hall I was overwhelmed with gratitude to God for placing Monica and Jacob in my life. It was a wake-up call, and I realized in those moments how fleeting life could be. I vowed that day to be a more patient and gracious husband and father. I thought of all the lonely people out there, the ones who haven't been lucky enough to find their match, or to bring new life into this world. Those were things that money couldn't buy, and they meant the world to me—more than any machine or purchase order or investment.

Time seemed to stand still, but slowly, very slowly, conversations changed as the clock ticked. The buzz around the hall began focusing on logistics as attendees heard that airports were closing right and left and flights were being canceled. The talk seemed to snap people out of their dazes, at least a little bit, and reminded them of what we were there for. Business didn't exactly go on as usual, but it did go on, accompanied by an overall sense of anxiety. It's not that people were worried so much about the effects of the tragedy on our industry. Not then. I don't think anyone really understood how something that happened in New York could affect us in Las Vegas. Mostly, the first few days after the attack were spent wondering if more attacks were about to hit America. A major tourist center like Las Vegas might be a prime secondary target for the terrorists.

But we all tried to push that to the back of our mind and go about our day-to-day routines. It wasn't easy, but to think about all the terrible possibilities could just drive you mad. So I managed to carry out my intended plans at the convention. I checked out the machine I'd come to see and it turned out to be exactly what I was hoping for. It cost about $50,000, and I ordered one. Believe it or not, it turned out to be a great investment, and one that my employees and I were actually able to operate pretty well. There was a first for everything.

But there was still one problem, and that was that the manufacturing machine wasn't going to do us much good if our packaging machine didn't work. And our packaging machine was on the brink of driving

me crazy, it had so many problems. I complained and complained to the
company, but nothing seemed to work.

Doboy, the company I bought it from, sent technicians on numer-
ous occasions, but to no avail. It got to the point where both Sam
and I agreed the situation was unbearable, and considering we paid
$125,000—which was more than twice the cost of the best normal hori-
zontal packaging machine they sold—the problem should be remedied.
They owed us that. After a series of angry phone calls and letters, they
finally relented and gave us full credit for the machine, and we used that
to fund a much simpler and much more effective one.

For about a full second the business was running smoothly. But before
I could even think about sitting back and resting on my laurels, I was
besieged with the greatest problem yet. And this time it had nothing to
do with my machines. It was a man named Dr. James Atkins.

Or, more precisely, the Atkins diet. You've probably heard about it;
most likely, you've even tried it. That was the diet that demonized car-
bohydrates and glorified fat and protein. It was the diet that said you
could eat bacon and cheese and have cream all day long, but they made
it sound like an ounce of an oat or a raisin could make you blow up like
a blimp. And it wasn't just Atkins; after that came South Beach and a
bunch of other low-carb trends.

After years of fat being bad and low fat or fat free being good, the
world had flipped upside down. The Oat Bar had very little fat in it. It
was by coincidence, not by design; but regardless, that's what its plat-
form had always been, and so it never had a problem fitting in with the
popular fitness trends. Suddenly, people were screaming at me that the
no-fat low-fat stuff was actually the root of the problem.

I always knew that the nutrition views of the American public and of
the fitness crowds had a tendency to shift as often as the fashion world.
So it was always in the back of my mind that something can be "in" and
then "out" in the blink of an eye.

But all of a sudden we were being hit with a one-two punch. In
addition to the protein obsession, the FDA made a new ruling on glycerin, which was one of the ingredients in my bars. Glycerin is a clear,

oil-like substance extracted from either vegetable or animal matter with a slightly sweet yet burning sensation if tasted alone. It's put in a variety of food products, as well as pharmaceuticals, cosmetics, soaps, and over-the-counter medicines to keep them soft, moist, and pliable. The substance also happened to be a carbohydrate, and the FDA ruling stated that it must be listed in the total carb count. So, not only did we have to deal with an already high carb count, we had to actually change our labels to reflect an even higher count that included the glycerin.

Sales tanked. They dropped nearly 70 percent. I let most of my workforce go and I felt like I was right back to square one, living off my credit cards and a dream. I fell back on what I'd learned in rehab and in meetings—the value of small steps and positive thinking. If there was any time to really dwell on those concepts, it was then.

I started making signs to put up all over the house and all over the plant that said, "I am going to overcome and prosper." It sounded small, but it was something that made me feel better. The old fake-it-till-you-make-it approach to a problem had always worked for me in the past. I knew that if I really believed in something and was willing to not only do the legwork but also put my faith in God and the universe, then all the forces would come together and make it happen. I knew that if I worked hard and prayed hard I could accomplish anything.

All I had to do was come up with a protein bar to sell, one that people loved even more than the Oat Bar, and I'd be set.

My investor wasn't quite so confident.

Sam started getting antsy. At this point he'd put about $300,000 into the company, and since we'd yet to turn a profit, he'd seen no return on his investment. On top of our sales tumbling, he'd also lost a lot in the stock market following 9/11. As a result, he tried to renegotiate our terms. Rather than discussing possible solutions, Sam used this sudden downturn for leverage. He told me that because my sales never got as high as he'd expected, and now that they had dropped, he was convinced that he should get a greater ownership stake than the 20 percent we agreed on. I told him I wasn't willing to budge on that. Nevertheless, we had no formal agreement laying out the terms of our financial relationship, so I guess you could say I was in a pickle.

I had Sam giving me the squeeze on one side, and on the other side, I had A Marketing draining me every month with no real results to show for it. On top of that, my old friend and distributor James was having the same problems I was because he couldn't get his stores to take high-carb products like they used to, including my bars. He wanted out of the business, so he gave me an ultimatum: I had to buy his customer list from him or face the loss of his sales. He wanted $135,000 for the list.

At this point a more rational person may have thrown in the towel, and it did cross my mind. They were all coming at me for money I didn't have and looking for controlling interest in a company that was bleeding money. But the bottom line was this: Oat Bars was my baby. Why would I hand it over to someone else when I was the one who had struggled and worked one-hundred-hour weeks for the previous seven years to see it grow and prosper?

Not sure what else was left to do, I asked God for a sign. And I got one.

Monica and I went to the movies, and in the lobby of the theater I saw one of those bear-claw machines filled with stuffed animals. My whole life I'd never been able to win one, but for some reason that day I was drawn to that machine. I put two quarters in and I said to myself, *God, if I am going to succeed in this business show me by letting me win a prize.*

I took the handle and moved the claw so it dangled just above the biggest prize in the machine—an orange, red, and white giraffe. I squinted at it, making sure it was lined up properly. Then I pressed the red button and the claw lowered right onto that giraffe. I knew at this point, however, that this was not a done deal. This was when most of the toys tumbled back into the machine. But as I watched, its grip held and it lifted . . . lifted . . . lifted . . . and held! The claw carried the giraffe over to the chute and dropped it in. I won!

As weird as it sounded, I actually felt a glow go through me, and then and there I knew everything was going to be all right. The answer was to keep control of the company and just keep working hard. One of the most important tenets of the path to self-made wealth is to retain as much of your own enterprise as you possibly can. That's what I would do. If I'd learned one thing from my days as an addict it was that when I did something, I did it full throttle. When I'm in, I'm in. And then and there, I was in.

So with renewed confidence I started making changes right and left. First, I terminated A Marketing. The returns I was getting just didn't justify the $3,000 to $5,000 a month I was spending on them. The next issue at hand was James. I couldn't afford to pay him the full $135,000, and I told him that, flat out. After going back and forth we ended up making a deal where I'd pay him $2,300 a month for five years in exchange for his list. Once I had access to the list I could cut out the middleman, and I could gross 50 percent more on those sales than before. That would shake out to a couple of thousand a month more than I had to pay James.

Regardless, I was pretty upset to be on the hook for all that money. Sure, James had helped me out back when I was struggling, but now he was just plain taking advantage. He was trying to get rich with no financial investment, and using me in the process. I'd done enough scheming in my day to know when I'd been had, but my hands were tied. I just had to play along.

Next up to bat was my relationship with Sam. That one was a little more complicated. When I wouldn't budge on giving him more control of the company, he started changing his story. With no contract stating that the $300,000 he'd sunk into the company had been investment dollars, he was trying to spin the situation and say that the money had actually been a loan to me, and now he wanted me to pay him all of that money back, with interest. I wasn't sure how to handle him, honestly. He threatened legal action if I didn't start making payments. When I didn't start making payments, he accused me of misleading him. That was what really got to me.

"I never, ever misled you," I told him. "I was straightforward from the beginning. I would have provided you with any information that was available, but you didn't bother doing any due diligence. If you never saw this as anything other than a loan, you never should have invested in the first place."

I was so mad. Not only had he fronted all this money as an "investor," I really had let him be a part of the company. I let him handle the packaging, work with artists, select machines. Through it all, something inside me thought that he was being bilked by all of those companies. I let it go because I figured it was his money, his decision. If I had known it would all come back to bite me in the form of an unauthorized loan, I never would have signed off on half the stuff he bought. At the same time, I knew that if he were to come after me legally, the fees would put me under.

I felt obligated to repay him, even if it wasn't exactly on my terms, so after a whole lot of pointless back and forth, I told him that I was willing to make arrangements. He said he wanted Monica and me to personally guarantee a large portion of the loan, and the rest would be in the form of the packaging machine, which he'd paid for. He said that what I owed him for that machine could be made into a lease. So, every month for the next fifteen years I would pay him $3,000, which covered the lease and the note and interest. I had no idea how I was going to pay him, but I didn't want to waste too much energy worrying about it. As always, I just had faith that everything was going to work out.

It was probably the most stressful period of my life, at least since I'd been sober. But never once did I consider picking up a drink or doing any kind of drug. If I knew one thing it was that my life, as it was, couldn't exist with alcohol or drugs in it. To take even a sip or a puff would mean throwing everything away.

Instead, work became my outlet, and when it wasn't work it was food. I fell back on my old childhood habit of turning to food for comfort. Stress made me eat more, and I kept piling on the pounds, so much so that I was diagnosed with Type 2 diabetes.

Monica worried about me and she worried about the business. She didn't have the same kind of blind faith I did, and she could see the toll that all of this was taking on me. I couldn't blame her for getting upset. She knew exactly the kind of shape we were in, the fact that I owed nearly $70,000 on my credit cards. She was right there beside me as we watched the company shrink from twelve employees to three part-timers. Many days she would come into the plant and help us out while Jacob watched us from his playpen. For years, she'd been patient and supportive. But this time she could see the storm clouds blowing in, and she suggested that I consider bankruptcy. I wouldn't hear it.

"You can't leave before the miracle happens," I told her.

CHAPTER 15

PART OF BEING POSITIVE meant putting the best spin on whatever situation I was in. So even as the financial pressures piled up around me, I came up with my own mantras. This was one of my favorites: "One thing that separates successful people from the rest is the ability or willingness to overcome obstacles." Inspirational phrases like that had a way of putting things in perspective.

I also continued reading anything and everything I could in the hope of learning something that would improve my situation. One of the magazines I picked up had a story about Henry J. Heinz, aka the ketchup magnate. That story really stuck with me because there were so many parts of it that I could relate to. See, Heinz didn't just know condiments—he knew business. And like any classic success story, his was full of struggles.

Henry founded Heinz Noble & Company in 1869 and sold horse-radish and pickles. An excellent salesman, he and his business partner, Clarence Noble, did well with the small company for a few years, until an oversupply of horseradish flooded the market and prices dropped drastically. In 1875 the company went bankrupt. Henry was flat broke and could barely afford to feed his family. He went to see the grocers he'd worked with for years, and they wouldn't even give him enough credit to take home the necessities.

Henry promised himself that he would never again be in a position in which he had to depend on others. Bankruptcy or no bankruptcy, he went back to the drawing board and started over. He was determined to be a success, and he knew that he could achieve anything he put his mind to. He vowed that he wouldn't stop until he got what he was after. "Our field is the world," he said.

It wasn't easy. Within a matter of months, according to newspaper accounts, he was selling his parents' furniture so he could settle liens on his equipment. Then he teamed up with a brother and a cousin (because of the bankruptcy Henry couldn't begin a venture on his own) and formed F & J Heinz, which began selling tomato ketchup (and more than fifty-seven other varieties, as the slogan goes). The company did well, and in 1888 Heinz bought out his other two partners and reorganized the company as the H. J. Heinz Company, the name it has to this day. Over the years, because of Henry's determintation and commitment, the business has become a $10 billion global corporation.

Heinz had reinvented himself and his focus after market forces pushed him to bankruptcy. With the public's sudden love affair with protein in the new century, I was faced with similar problems. I believed that if I could devise the right protein-rich formula, I could be to protein bars what Heinz is to ketchup. One of Henry's quotes that really stuck with me was, "Do not sell yourself short, the world is waiting."

He was right. The world *was* waiting. It had taken years to build all the right connections in all the right places, and now they were all vying for me. I had the equipment, the business know-how, and the right location. The stars were all perfectly aligned. Now I just needed to come up with the right recipe.

I started researching proteins. I found that a combination of whey and soy resulted in the creamiest consistency. Add to that the naturally occurring protein from the oats and my bar would have three different proteins in it. I figured the more sources the better. Once I had that down, I started experimenting with fat. I had more leeway this time around because fat was no longer the enemy. I could at least add oil as a liquid.

I must have gone through nearly a hundred different recipes trying to find the perfect versions of two new flavors: chocolate coconut and peanut butter chocolate chip. Then I wrapped them all up and waited to see what happened as they aged. This was the big test.

After a few weeks passed I checked on the results. Some of the bars ended up getting moldy, others were too dry, some were too crumbly, and most often, the taste just wasn't quite there. But there were a few that really grabbed my palate. They were rich, flavorful, protein-packed, moist, and shelf stable. I did a bunch of taste tests to figure out which one of the finalists had best flavor, and then I sent samples out to my distributors, along with a questionnaire for comments.

Their responses were really encouraging: "Great tasting." "I would buy it!" "Filling." "Tastes like real food." Only one person suggested that I bury the bars in the backyard. The funny thing is, years down the line that guy ended up buying a whole lot of bars, and he's still my customer to this day.

I hadn't come up with a name for the new bars yet, so I was asking everyone I met—from my distributors to store managers to my employees at Chef Jay's Food Products—for input. It was actually the young woman who was working part-time as my secretary who suggested the name Trioplex.

"Why Trioplex?" I asked her.

"The 'tri' stands for the three kinds of protein in the bar," she said. "The 'o' would be because it's an oat-based bar, and 'plex' because it's all blended together."

It was perfect. All I did was add a hyphen to separate the three parts and there you had it: Tri-O-Plex.

I didn't want to hire a graphic artist to conceptualize the logo this time around. From what I'd seen over the years, I was just as capable of producing the design, so after walking through the grocery store and noting which products caught my eye and which didn't, I bought some colored pencils and drawing paper and mocked something up. It doesn't get more mom-and-pop than that, does it?

I found a design firm willing to take on the project, and for less than $10,000 I was able to do everything—film design, plates, all of it. That was more than $90,000 cheaper than when Sam had managed the logo, which proved my worries had been right on.

Monica and I discussed how we would fund it all. My sales that July were the lowest they'd been in years. There was just no money coming in. All of my hopes lay in the introduction of the new Tri-O-Plex bar, but first I had to be able to afford to make it. I found out that I qualified for a home equity line of credit for around $25,000, which was just the amount I needed. I told Monica that, and she was supportive, but worried. She told me that if this didn't work I should consider throwing in the towel.

"You have to know when to quit," I remember her telling me.

I agreed with her, but in my own mind quitting was never an option. Even though I knew that if we lost this, we lost everything.

♦

My goal was to have the first run completed in time for the 2002 Mr. Olympia bodybuilding show, which also involved a trade show. My bars were perfect for the bodybuilding crowd. Not only were they teeming with protein but, at 118 grams, they were the biggest bar on the market, compared to the more common size of 78 grams.

Bodybuilders themselves were great marketers. If they found something they liked they were going to tell their friends and their local stores about it. Knowing full well that this could make or break me, I went all in. I arranged to have a promotional gym bag to give away, and to ensure that the distributors actually came to my booth, I sent out letters telling them they had to RSVP if they wanted this bag. I heard back from close to three-quarters of them saying they'd be there.

I made five thousand bars in preparation: twenty-five hundred each of the chocolate coconut and the peanut butter chocolate chip. The night before the show I had them all boxed and ready to hand out, along with the bags and the flyers. All that was left to do was to say a little prayer.

The day of the show I was nervous. I'd lost a lot of sleep over this moment, and it was finally here. I could feel the pressure, but that was always something that had driven me even harder. I hadn't come this far to sweat and flub my lines.

Looking around me, I tried to put the stress aside and take it all in. Not everyone gets the chance to check out a bodybuilding convention, and I felt pretty lucky to be a part of it. Hulking, tanned, glistening people were all around me. Famous people, like Arnold Schwarzenegger, Lou Ferrigno, Olympia contenders, and actors from "Baywatch," walked among them. The muscles were big, and the egos were sometimes even bigger than the physiques. Everyone milled around the booths, checking out the supplements and the apparel.

As the Strongman Competition went on across the convention hall, I handed out samples to everyone, and I mean everyone, from bodybuilders to distributors to your normal everyday Joe. The responses were similar to the ones I'd gotten from the stores. Folks thought my new bars were delicious, and a nice change from the usual protein bar that uses candy coating to disguise the awful taste and texture beneath. I put on my salesman hat and talked up Tri-O-Plex as best I could.

I got a bunch of commitments for orders, which I followed up on after the show. The commitments held strong, and just one month later, at the end of October, I had $12,000 in sales. That number doubled in November, to $24,000, which surpassed our Oat Bar sales that month by $4,000. Even as the winter approached, sales showed no signs of slowing. December's sales of Tri-O-Plex were $35,000, which when added to the still-flat sales of Oat Bars, made for my best month in more than a year. Not bad, considering December was usually the slowest month and we took two weeks off for the holidays.

It was unprecedented. I had distributors buying a pallet at a time and selling it in less than a week. They could barely keep them on their shelves, and we were cranking them out as fast as we could to fill the orders. The money just kept rolling in. In January the sales of Tri-O-Plex reached $55,000. Together with my other sales, that added up to $95,000, which was the best month I'd had since I opened the shop. I finally started paying off some of the debt I had amassed.

In February the sales of the Tri-O-Plex soared to $98,000, bringing in a net monthly total of $130,000. As it became more clear that the orders weren't a fluke, they were going to remain consistent, I started making some changes and putting the money I'd been making back into the company. I hired a couple of people to help me out. James, my old distributor pal, came on as a salesman and I hired a plant manager. They handled the day-to-day issues while I focused on manufacturing. It gave me a chance to come up with a new Tri-O-Plex flavor, Smores, which we launched in March and helped give sales even more of a turbo boost. By the end of May, monthly sales were up to $290,000, even though the Oat Bar sales dwindled back to about $20,000.

In less than a year, I'd gone from being on the brink of financial ruin to this. Reflecting back on it all, I thought about the hours I'd put in, the backbreaking labor, the sleepless nights, the endless sweat equity, and how, finally, one day at a time, it was starting to pay off.

I didn't realize it at the time, but I think I actually drew on a lot of strength that came from the days when I was so steeped in my addictions. I think the thing that separated me from so many other people was that I was unwilling to quit. I just wouldn't hear of it. I attributed that to my past. I had failed at or quit so many things I had attempted earlier in my life before I got sober that I had grown used to it. Grown to expect it even, and I certainly had no fears about it. For so much of my life I'd had nothing to lose, and that was ingrained in my mind-set. Ultimately, if I didn't succeed, well that was just nothing new.

◆

The larger the business grew the more issues I had with my employees. Sometimes they just up and left, which was really just a reflection of the nature of a transient city like Las Vegas. Other times were more dramatic, like the guy who started sleeping with one of my other employees, who happened to be married with children. The two of them ended up leaving the plant (and, I think, the state) at the same time. But even with the high turnover, business remained strong, with sales in June hitting $375,000. Watching those numbers go up, up, up still felt like peering into another man's life.

I really didn't even spend much of the money. I was so happy to be able to get back in the black that the thought of buying something extravagant didn't even cross my mind. The honest truth is I didn't know how long the glory days would last, so I thought it was a good idea to save whatever I made.

Mainly I kept focusing on growing the business. I introduced a new Tri-O-Plex flavor in July—caramel apple—to help summer sales and avoid the typical summer slump. People had a tendency to focus more on their vacations than their diets in the summer, and I needed to do everything in my power to entice them to keep up with the protein bars. It worked. Sales kept growing through August and September, and by October they had more than doubled again, to $861,000.

Time was passing by in a blur. My head was perpetually spinning. I was amazed by the influx of orders, but more than anything I was just out and out busy all the time. I worked endless hours just to try to keep up with it all. When I'd moved into the new building, I thought five thousand square feet would be too much space. But with all the rapid growth, we quickly filled any and all of the space we had.

By the end of 2003 we had done more than $4 million in sales. That was ten times the amount we did in 2002. In desperate need of space, I ended up leasing the suite next door to the plant and knocked a hole in the wall so we could run a conveyor belt through there and add on more equipment to make more bars. Then the next suite emptied out and I leased that one and did the same thing. I just kept expanding sideways, and before I knew it I'd taken over nine suites and had conveyor belts running up into the ceiling, through walls, making turns. We were running power from one suite to another to keep it all moving, and after a while even that wasn't enough, so I ended up buying power from the church that was our neighbor. With space so tight, I set up a storage area about four or five miles away. I did whatever I needed to do to make it work.

January started with a bang. James had a contact in Canada that loved the bars so much they bought an entire truckload of them and sold them throughout the country. From there, our name snowballed to a new, international audience, and we were contacted by people in the England, Australia, Israel, Turkey, Belgium, Denmark, Poland, Spain, and Brazil. We managed to sell $1.7 million that month and $1.3 million the following month. I was astounded. Over and over again, astounded. Each month I looked at the books in disbelief, expecting it all to end. I mean, just a few months earlier, I had hoped to do a million in sales for the entire year. Now I'd done that and more in a single month—twice!

I finally started feeling comfortable enough to spend some of the money. I wanted to do something nice for Monica. We'd never had a honeymoon, so I flew her mother up to watch Jacob for a week and took Monica on a cruise to the Mediterranean.

I also started investing some of the money in real estate. I knew that was a sound place for growth, and in Las Vegas there were all sorts of foreclosed properties available. I started buying them up, refurbishing them, and renting them out to low-income residents. It was satisfying work, taking a house that was abandoned and in most cases destroyed, and working on it so it could be habitable again. It was kind of the theme of own my life. I'd reinvented myself, reinvented my business, and this was a way of reinventing a house and sharing the end product with others. Plus, in a place known for its lack of affordable housing, it was a much-needed service. On top of that, it made good business sense, because whatever rent I charged paid off the mortgage and then some. For someone who had spent half of his life looking for a place to crash, it felt pretty good. Everyone came out a winner.

I bought a new home for my family. The area where we'd been living had really gone downhill in ten years. The last straw was when a little boy was shot and killed at a nearby park, a place where Monica liked to jog and often took Jacob in a stroller. I couldn't stand the thought of putting them at risk.

So we bought our dream home (or so we thought at the time). It was nearly four thousand square feet, located within a gated community in an exclusive part of Henderson, adjacent to Las Vegas. I bought all new furniture for the place, set up a game room with a pool table, jukebox, full-sized arcade games, a popcorn machine, massage chair, and two built-in surround-sound entertainment centers. I paid for it all in cash.

It was weird, adjusting to having money. I had been living hand to mouth for so long I hardly knew what it was like to live any differently. Like I said, I always knew I'd be successful. But I guess my idea of success was that I'd be making $70,000 or $80,000 a year and I'd be happy. Well, we were just a couple of months into the year and I'd probably already surpassed that imagined annual salary. My earlier modest dreams were probably the reason why I never got overly extravagant in the ways I would spend the money. We started traveling more and dining out, and I did walk into a jeweler's with a wad of cash and buy that Rolex. But mostly we just lived comfortably.

I always knew that if I believed in myself the universe would make it happen for me. So I kept on believing and those sales just kept rising. In March we sold $1.5 million, and in April it was $1.8 million. Distributors were putting second and third orders in before they even received their first. At the plant we always had two shifts going strong, and it wasn't uncommon for us to crank out bars twenty-four hours a day. It seemed like there was no end in sight.

As Tri-O-Plex sales soared, Oat Bar sales continued tanking. In May they dropped all the way down to $2,000, and it was no longer economically feasible to continue making them. Not when their production was taking away from the protein bars. Years earlier I had taken the ax to the muffins. It was finally time to do the same to the Oat Bar.

CHAPTER 16

ALTHOUGH THE BUILDUP TO my success had taken years, it felt like it hit overnight. The days when I was hocking a gold coin to take my wife out to dinner were a distant memory. Now I was flying around the country in a private jet, living in my dream home, and buying up real estate right and left. I was a multimillionaire by the end of 2004.

Sales stayed so high that I moved out of my conjoined office suites and bought my own building, which was a little over eighteen thousand square feet. I put on a second level, even though the builder said I couldn't and the city made me put in an elevator. I built my dream office overlooking the plant. I also leased the building next door (because the builder would not sell it), which gave us a total of forty-five thousand square feet.

I spent around $2 million on new equipment. We're talking custom-designed futuristic-style robotics and conveyor belts that could spin out up to two hundred bars a minute—four times the amount our old machines could handle. It eliminated worker contact with the bars, which actually helped improve their quality. This time around I made sure that I saw it working properly before any check was signed. I'd finally learned that lesson.

I also assembled a full-time tech team that could deal with problems as they arose. No more waiting for the manufacturing company to send out reps. I didn't have time for that kind of stuff anymore. No, I was too busy becoming the Henry J. Heinz of protein bars, just as I'd dreamed.

As the sales came in and the bars went out with alarming speed, I had to admit I was beginning to feel invincible. Even for a recovering addict, this kind of high was unlike any I'd experienced in my whole life.

I was so caught up in it that I forgot to consider the lesson I'd learned all those years ago, the lesson that seemed to apply, without fail, to drugs, gravity, and egos: what goes up must come down.

Once summer hit Las Vegas and temperatures soared well into the triple digits, I started having some issues with trucking companies. All the vehicles were so busy carting California produce back and forth across the country I could hardly flag them down in Vegas to transport my products. When they did make the stop, it was ridiculously expensive. So I figured I was better off just starting my own trucking company.

I bought all new trucks. Four of them: beautiful, shiny Volvos with new refrigerator trailers. Each one cost me a little under $200,000, and somehow that price tag was the least of my headaches.

The problem actually had nothing to do with my own products. I never had an issue keeping the trucks loaded with bars. I could send them out across the country as fast as they would go. The problem was getting enough return loads to justify the cost of the operation. I couldn't consistently find enough products for the trucks to haul back toward Las Vegas, and even when I did find stuff, the brokers were too cheap to deal with. My own drivers were also getting impatient waiting around. Add to that the skyrocketing gas prices, and it was pretty rough on the profit margin.

On top of all that, there was a whole new set of people and problems to deal with. Take this one driver who, on his maiden voyage, took the truck and drove off with it. Just disappeared. We called him on his cell phone and some other guy answered it. "Oh, I don't know who that is. This guy just sold me his phone for like $70."

Turned out the driver was selling the product off the back of the truck in east Dallas in the middle of some parking lot. We went and retrieved the truck, and that's when I realized that maybe the trucking business wasn't worth the years it was taking off my life.

That was my first company that didn't take off. Then there was my first product that ran into some real problems: The world's first self-heating soup. If it sounds too good to be true, well, apparently it was. But that was something I had to learn the hard way.

I'd seen Wolfgang Puck coffee that was in a self-heating can made by a company called OnTech, and I thought how great that would be if applied to a high-protein soup. I came up with three flavors—hearty beef, zesty chicken, and French onion—and OnTech developed the container. I signed a long-term contract saying that I would buy x amount of soup over the next few years. After making so many business decisions that didn't include contracts, I thought that this was the right thing to do. I was tired of being jerked around.

So I started talking to my contacts about the soup, and everybody wanted it, all the major retailers. It was cutting-edge technology, high protein, and the first of its kind. What's not to love?

The soup rolled out, and next thing I heard was that the containers were leaking. There was something wrong with the cans—they weren't working right—and the retailers were not happy. Turned out that the cans of Wolfgang Puck coffee were having the same problem. I told OnTech I didn't want to buy a product associated with Chef Jay's Foods that was clearly a failure (although my words were not quite that nice). In the meantime, I tried to make good with all the retailers by reimbursing them for the unacceptable soup.

OnTech came after me with a lawsuit. They weren't budging from the contract I'd signed. Like it or not, I was committed to buying a whole lot of soup over the next few years, and they didn't seem to care whether their product leaked. I tried to arrive at some kind of settlement with them, but they wouldn't even listen.

Between the expense of reimbursing all the stores and the threat of a lawsuit, I knew I was up against a possible bankruptcy. All the progress

I had made looked like it was about to be washed down the drain like a leaky can of soup.

Then the FDA stepped in and announced a voluntary recall of more than a dozen self-heating products made by OnTech, including my soup. That was both good and bad. It was good because, ultimately, it got me out of my contract. But now that there was a recall, I was responsible for compensating each and every customer that had bought the soup, and I was also responsible for the destruction of any cans of soup that remained on the market. Considering that the first production run amounted to nearly 250,000 cans, this was no small task.

Once it was all said and done, I was out nearly $1 million. But I still had my company, at least, and I still had my never-say-die positive attitude. I was never bitter about that soup venture—or the truck venture, for that matter. I learned something from each attempt, and that was that you could and should try anything, you just had to know when to say when. Know your strengths, but also know your weaknesses. These challenges reminded me of my weaknesses at a time when I really needed to hear it.

The wealth had come so fast that without even realizing it I had turned into a real jerk. It kind of went to my head, and I lost sight of who I was. I had become very controlling at work and around the house, barking orders and acting holier than thou. I guess I thought that because I was now a millionaire I had this newfound sense of superiority and thought I could do no wrong.

Fact of the matter was that I could and did do a whole lot of wrong. Every issue that got in my way brought me down a notch and handed my humility right back to me. I'll admit that in the moment I wasn't always grateful for that return to humility, but in the long run I sure was.

◆

On July 6, 2006, Monica gave birth to Isaiah, our second son. This pregnancy was entirely different—no bed rest, no bleeding, nothing.

Isaiah was a big baby, 9 pounds, and all three of us, Monica, Jacob, and I, were so happy to have a new member of the family.

I admit it took me awhile to get used to the idea of kids and adjusted to having the little ones around. Mostly I had to accept that it was up to me to be a good father, not up to my past, not up to my DNA. I made a conscious decision to have a good relationship with my boys. I'm a pretty stoic guy, but it's something that I get emotional talking about, even thinking about. I would do anything for those kids.

One thing that my boys helped me realize was that I really needed to lose weight. My job had become its own occupational hazard. Sure I was making healthy products, but it was my duty to taste all of those, hundreds of times over, until they were right. Ever since culinary school my weight had steadily been increasing. Chasing after the kids gave me a whole new perspective on my limitations.

There was one time we took a trip to Lego Land. Jacob wanted to go on some carnival-type ride that had one of those metal bars you pull down over your waist as a seat belt. Well, I climbed into the ride with him and tried to put that bar down, only to find it wouldn't budge. I was too big. I was humiliated when they told me I couldn't ride the ride.

And it wasn't just that. I'd been kicked off planes because they said I was too fat, I barely fit in chairs in the movie theater, and it was all starting to take a toll on my health. My doctor had put me on two kinds of insulin for my diabetes, and the medicine contributed to an 80-pound weight gain, which brought me up to 416 pounds—more than I'd ever weighed in my life. I was also on four oral diabetes pills, as well as drugs for high cholesterol, acid reflux, and high blood pressure.

It was getting harder and harder just to do normal, everyday activities. It all came to a head when I was attempting to bend over and tie my shoelaces, and I could barely do it. I ended up gasping for breath, helpless. I flashed back sixteen years to the moment in the 19th Hole when I'd sworn off drinking. I realized I felt about the same way at this moment as I did when I was strung out on drugs and alcohol. My limitations were so severe that the world was just passing me by.

I don't want to live like this, I thought to myself. *I'm done.* And I vowed that it was time to change my life again.

So, as I worked on getting my business back on its feet, I did the same thing for myself. Just like there was no magical cure for my addictions, weaning myself off of food and embracing a healthier lifestyle would have to be a gradual process. My first priority was focusing on fitness. I knew I had to find a workout that I liked or I wouldn't do it.

I figured out a plan that would help me burn the most calories and increase muscle. I started running on a treadmill every morning, doing twenty minutes a day, at least three days a week, at my target heart rate. I calculated my maximum heart rate (175) which was 220 minus my age. Then I made daily workout goals. At first I aimed for 50 percent of my maximum heart rate; gradually I built up to 75 percent, and then 85 percent. I made it a part of my routine. I worked out in the morning on an empty stomach. I would just grab my tea (I prefer tea to coffee for the health benefits, and I'm not tempted by any calorie-laden creamer), put on my headphones, and listen to some hard rock music as I monitored my heart rate through a heart monitor. Twenty minutes. Anyone can make that time commitment, as long as you find a workout you like.

On top of that, I lifted weights in the afternoon. That helped me build lean muscle mass, which, in turn, burns fat (as opposed to plain old fat, which does not burn fat itself.) I knew that it was important to go about it all properly. It's possible to be a so-called normal weight and still have a lot of fat, and I didn't want to see that happen. My goal was to be fit, healthy, and sports-car ready. That's right. To motivate myself, I put a picture of this smoking-hot Ferrari I wanted in front of the treadmill.

When I lose all this weight I'm going to buy this car, I promised myself. Ever since I was a kid I had loved cars. I had always wanted an exotic sports car, but I could never fit in one. My stomach would get in the way of the steering wheel.

Turned out it was just the motivation I needed. That picture made me work even harder. I knew it would. It put me in the zone. Of course, not everyone can bait him- or herself with a Ferrari, and it doesn't have to be that extreme. It can be as simple as a new pair of pants or a new dress in a smaller size, a trip to Disneyland, or the ability to run a marathon—whatever. The important thing is to reward yourself, and to use whatever tools you have to accomplish your goal. Just like a mechanic needs tools to work on a car, we need tools to work on ourselves. That Ferrari was *some* tool.

I knew that in addition to working out I needed to start eating differently. I was usually so busy all day that I wouldn't eat much, and then I'd go home and find that Monica had cooked a huge meal for dinner. We'd have fried chicken, for example, and then I'd snack and go to sleep. It was about the worst thing I could be doing to myself.

I didn't want to try some kind of diet because I knew I'd fail. In my mind, a diet was no different from a temporary distraction. What I needed was a complete overhaul of my relationship with food. I had relied on it for all the wrong reasons for too long. I ate out of stress, out of emotion, and out of habit. I couldn't just put a bandage over those behaviors; I had to change them. I had to reshape my views and see food as something that gave me energy, not happiness and not escape.

I started eating small (six ounces or less), high-protein portions throughout the day. I would eat five or six times a day, every two to three hours, because that's how you boost your metabolism. It's important to control your appetite. I really tried to stay away from sugar. Sugar-free gelatin was helpful because it's basically no calories and gives you a full feeling; you can eat as much as you want. I would also eat one of my fifty-gram bars and drink an eight-ounce glass of water before meals to give myself that full feeling, at only around a hundred calories. Once in a while I would eat one of my cookies, and then I developed my high-protein Lite Bite cookies with reduced sugar and calories.

There are some people who use various bariatric surgeries to control their appetites. I cannot endorse any particular tool because it needs to be a personal preference and you have to decide what works best for you. There are various complications associated with the different surgical options available, and they are always changing. But realize that there is no magic bullet with the particular tools you use.

There is a high failure rate with anything that requires hard work. The secret is to take these tools and make them work and ignore the failure statistics. Tell yourself the statistics don't apply to you. Do you think anyone would go into business if they thought the failure rate of new businesses applied to them? Or what about the statistic that only one in thirty-three people who get sober stay sober? If you listened to those statistics would you even try? But I know many people who have been successful in new businesses and many more who have stayed sober. According to the numbers, the success stories likely had odds stacked against them in the millions to one. But not one of those successes thought those numbers applied to them, and they made it happen.

For me, the weight just melted off. Week after week, month after month, my body started totally morphing, and my energy was as high as it had ever been. Through it all sales stayed up and I kept introducing new products, like high-protein cookies and brownies, and they did well too. It was a lot to keep up with, and I needed all the energy I could get.

I had hit my stride: my business life was soaring, my family life was soaring, and everything was looking up. I had established some really solid relationships with all of my vendors. But, being the perpetual deal maker that I am, I was always on the lookout for a better bargain. My recipes always remained consistent, but the ingredients would sometimes come from different places according to the best prices offered. For instance, when a company in Georgia approached me with some aggressive pricing on their peanuts and peanut butter, I signed on. I'd dealt with the company before, so I really didn't give it a second thought. In September 2008, I started buying from them in bulk and using both products in my bars.

Through no fault of my own, I quickly learned that I'd made what was maybe the biggest mistake in my career. See, the company I'd bought the peanut products from was called The Peanut Corporation of America. You've probably heard of it. That's the company that, in January 2009, was embroiled in one of the largest food scares in history. Traces of salmonella were found in their peanuts and peanut butter, and eventually, we learned that at least on twelve occasions they knowingly sent out tainted product that had failed food safety tests. They sold their products to countless companies across the globe, and billions of products were possibly contaminated.

For months sales plummeted and people across the country fell ill from eating products with peanuts in them. More than six hundred people became sick, and eight died from what appeared to be salmonella poisoning, although not one case was conclusively tied to the tainted peanut butter. Still, it was a disaster. In all, more than eighteen hundred product lines across the nation were recalled, including my cookies and bars that had peanut butter in them. Thank God, no one who ate my products became ill.

When the FDA announced a recall, we had to handle the crisis in the same way we handled the soup recall. It was our responsibility both to reimburse anyone who had purchased our products and to remove any potentially tainted products from the marketplace. I knew I wouldn't be able to live with the idea of my products making someone sick, so I did anything and everything within my power to destroy those bars, and I hired an outside company to certify that I had done so. The whole ordeal will probably cost more than $1 million, but the final numbers are not in at the time of this writing. And even though I took care of it in the most effective way possible, my company's reputation would still suffer, as would the reputation of any company that sold any products with peanuts in them, regardless of their origin. Something that took years to build would now take years to repair.

I handled it the way I always handled things. I smiled through the stress and kept my thoughts positive and my head up. If I could just do that, I knew everything would be okay, and as time passed it would become a distant memory.

Exercise really became an outlet for me during the hard times. Whatever problems I was dealing with, once I was on that treadmill staring at the picture of that Ferrari, I got right back into the zone. After a year of changing my eating habits and working out, the diabetes was gone; it was the same with the high blood pressure and the high cholesterol. I was off all medications. The only thing I took was nutritional supplements. Not only that, but I'd lost right around 200 pounds and had got down to just 14 percent body fat. I was a new man in so many ways.

I bought that 2008 Ferrari F430 Spider, just like I'd told myself I would. Ferraris are not easy to get. Normally, there's a three- to five-year wait to get one new, and the challenge was part of the attraction to me. I had to do some finagling, but somehow they let me slide by, and I bought one new from the factory in classic silver.

Like I said, if you want something badly enough, work hard, think positively, and put your faith in God and you'll get it.

CHAPTER 17

THANKFUL FOR ALL OF my successes, all of my blessings, and my sheer luck, I've decided these days that it's time to give back. One of my main focuses is nutrition for kids. I see the menu at Jacob's elementary school—pizza and chicken nuggets and all these high-fat foods—and then they're cutting back on physical education and wondering why kids are so over-weight. When it comes to things like that, I'm proud to be in a position where I can step in and help. Someone's got to do something.

So, I'm a big supporter of a nonprofit program called Chefs for Kids. It's a collaboration between the University of Nevada Cooperative Extension and the Las Vegas chapter of the American Culinary Federation, and its mission is to educate the community about nutrition and to fight hunger in kids. I donated nine thousand Lite Bite Chocolate Chip Cookies to twelve elementary schools throughout Las Vegas and North Las Vegas, and each child got to eat one of my healthy cookies. I hope to get more involved with that kind of stuff in years to come.

I know I couldn't have gotten where I am without the help of the recovery community. Through the years I've continued to take part in meetings, sharing my story in the hope of inspiring others.

It's nice to return to my roots. Even though I'm still in the food industry, there's a huge distance between me and my customers. I rarely, if
ever, get to see the reaction on people's faces when they try my products for the first time. That's something I've always loved about my job,
and I really miss it. So, I returned to my roots by taking some burners
over to a halfway house, buying a hundred or so eggs and a bunch of
toppings—bacon, mushrooms, onions, ham, and cheese—and offering
a little buffet of made-to-order omelets.

Most of the people don't know me from Adam. I blend in there,
wearing my workout shorts or sweat pants and the sleeveless navy blue
"Chef Jay's Food Products" T-shirt I wear everywhere. I take orders
and I cook.

"Are you a server for a living?" is one of the questions I often get.

"I make products, protein bars and cookies," I'll answer. "I just do
this to keep in practice, in case I ever have to go get a job."

As much as I'm there to help them, those weekend mornings are also
a big help to me. They're a reminder of where I came from and all that
I've overcome.

Sure, my life is different now. I'm down to eight percent body fat.
I've just moved into my approximately six-thousand-square-foot dream
home on a half acre of land located in one of the most exclusive com-
munities near Las Vegas (as it turned out, that four-thousand-square-
foot house wasn't quite dreamy enough, although it felt like it at the
time). In my new house, the kitchen alone is a thousand square feet. The
house has eleven TVs, a home theater, jukebox, full-sized golf machine,
pinball machine, and just about anything else you can imagine. And
then there's my car collection. In addition to a limited edition 2009
Ferrari F430 Scuderia (the fastest Ferrari convertible ever built), I've got
a Hummer 2, a Cadillac Escalade, a customized F250 Ford 100th anniversary Lariat truck, and a Lamborghini LP560 Spyder.

But the thing is this: Anybody can do what I've done. Anybody can
change his or her life. And that's what I tell people at the halfway house.
Just the other day I was talking to someone who was just ten days out

of prison. He happened to see the car I was driving, and I told him that anything is possible.

"I came from nothing," I said. "And you can do that too. You can be an inspiration to people."

The recipe for success is pretty simple: Go for it. Even when all odds seem to be against you and getting ahead seems less likely than winning the lottery, go for it. Don't give up. Chase after it like you've got nothing to lose, because everything pales in comparison to what you stand to gain. It worked for me with getting sober, and then it worked for my company, and then it worked for my weight loss and health. Along the way I had a lot of challenges, but those are what made me who I am today. People say that you learn more from your failures than you do your successes, and I believe that.

You have to try to go after your dreams. The worst thing you can do is just sit around and get old and say *I never tried all those things I wanted to do*. I'm going to be able to say I tried them. Maybe they didn't all work, but at least I tried. A lot of people see stubbornness as a bad thing. I see it as a key to success.

But it's not the key to happiness. My family is as important to me as any financial success I've had. Without them it would all be pointless. I've worked hard to have a relationship with each of my sons that makes us all happy. Every night when I come home I have an imaginary hat rack out in the garage that I hang all of my work problems and frustrations on. I walk inside and my boys light up. I show up for all their games and practices and school events, and I just love being an important part of their lives.

I think back over all those years ago, when Monica and I were working ourselves to the bone, with no returns, and she was crying and asking me to just take on a normal job. Back then I told her, "You can't leave before the miracle happens."

At the time I had no idea how many miracles there were in store for us. My wife and I both agree that every single one of them has been worth the wait.

ABOUT THE AUTHOR

JAY LITTMANN SPENT THE years between the ages of twelve and twenty-nine walking through a drunken, drug-addled haze. He turned away from his affluent family, his friends, and his future until, one day, he decided he'd had enough.

From there he began his inspirational journey to becoming a chef. Through countless battles he built his multimillion-dollar company, Chef Jay's Food Products. Along the way he discovered the value of love, through his wife, Monica, and the meaning of life, through his sons, Jacob and Isaiah.

Chef Jay and his family live in Henderson, Nevada, where he frequently shares his message of hope with others who battle addiction.